Atheism
Reclaimed

Atheism Reclaimed

Patrick O'Connor

BOOKS

Winchester, UK
Washington, USA

First published by iff Books, 2014
iff Books is an imprint of John Hunt Publishing Ltd., Laurel House, Station Approach,
Alresford, Hants, SO24 9JH, UK
office1@jhpbooks.net
www.johnhuntpublishing.com
www.iff-books.com

For distributor details and how to order please visit the 'Ordering' section on our website.

Text copyright: Patrick O'Connor 2013

ISBN: 978 1 78279 652 7

A CIP catalogue record for this book is available from the British Library.

Design: Stuart Davies

Printed and bound by CPI Group (UK) Ltd, Croydon, CR0 4YY

CONTENTS

For Frances McGeehan – as promised once on the Salmon Weir Bridge in Galway.

Introduction

Atheism has lost its soul; contemporary atheism is losing its vitality and it needs to reaffirm it. What is called atheism has lost vibrancy, mattering less and less. It is not relevant to understanding the nihilistic drive to destruction that is affecting all aspects of human experience from political organization, to the environment, to overpopulation. Personal proclamations of atheism and the attendant scientific appeals to evidence, questioning, humanism and critique are simply not relevant. Atheism needs to get its house in order. The task is to give a vital and positive account of atheism. Atheism cannot simply be a negation, but must take a position in its own right with positive philosophical consequences.

When American President Barack Obama gave his Inauguration Speech in 2008 he included reference to atheists. This was rightly celebrated and most welcome. It was, however, a limited reference in that it defined atheism as just another existing stakeholder in society, an option among many potential lifestyle choices. Without doubt its mention was a progressive step in highlighting the importance of atheism for public discourse; however, it did not go far enough, as it evacuated atheism of its potential for universal appeal. This book is an attempt to remedy this situation by offering two things. Firstly, in an effort to present a radical atheism, I would like this text to encourage dialogue within atheism in an effort to help it revitalize itself. Secondly, the text attempts to create a grammar of a more radical atheism, as well as an appeal to atheists to transform their existing practices.[1] Too often atheism is smug and complacent, hiding behind critique, criticism and appeals to evidence as if they were only meaningful in themselves. I would like to make the case for using the resources of an alternative lineage of thinkers to construct a new form of radicalised atheism. This will involve gleaning insights from Karl Marx, Friedrich Nietzsche, Martin Heidegger, Jean-Paul Sartre, Paolo Virno, and Jacques Rancière among others. However, I sincerely address this text to all and in good cheer. It is not intended to condemn or condone, merely to open up a possible space of discourse to help atheism become more relevant to human life.

The question of relevance is important. Without wanting to denounce the totality of what I call scientific or materialist atheism, which is to say the atheism based on the evidential explorations of science – as best evidenced in the writings of Sam Harris, Richard Dawkins and Daniel Dennett – I would claim that in terms of the real existential and political realities that are currently facing the world, these intellectual gambits are sorely lacking. Life – existence – is becoming increasingly cheap: culture is slowly eroding, entrepreneurial life is hollowing out meaning, and political life itself is worth nothing. In this malaise, it is as if nothing is any longer worthy of fidelity or commitment, and that this is happening in countries that have been most notably bequeathed the Enlightenment legacy is most worrying. For the scientific atheist, here is a truth worth heeding. The political and social clout of what has recently been called 'new atheism' has obviously failed to grab the imagination of large swathes of the populace. This is because one can only be committed to meaningful political interventions. A call for reason and scientific inquiry does not galvanize populations, nor does it provide a remedy to the rise of nihilism which is so often associated, fairly or not, with the centrality of science to intellectual life. With respect to the aforementioned authors, their work only takes us so far. When one thinks of overpopulation, the melting ice-caps, war and genocide, the atheist is not the first person one thinks of calling. Certainly it might be argued that the scientist is the best person to approach on climate change, but not in terms of the lived factuality of humans existing in the world, who have to grapple daily with the enormity of these undeniable problems.

Moreover, atheism does not feature in most political manifestos, economic discussions to solve the financial crisis, or with regard to any policy on public health. The scientific materialist may argue that the world would be a better place if scientists were put in charge of our governments, but in terms of real world problems the ethos of scientific materialism is strikingly ossified as a galvanizing force with purpose. This is because there is a serious disjunction between the meaning of scientific expertise and the vagaries of human reality. However, still, this book is not a critique of scientific atheism, but an attempt both to transgress and to complement it with a more profound atheism.

In philosophical terms, we can trace the source of the split between scientific and humanist accounts of the human to the oft-unspoken split between existential and scientific atheism; a split that in philosophical circles has played itself out in the rivalries between European and Analytic Philosophy. For this reason, Stephen Hawking's recent proclamation of the death of philosophy ought to sound more caustic to analytic ears than it does to continental philosophers.[2] The reason for such comparative ease and unease is instructive. Analytic philosophy has prided itself on its rigour and its contribution to the progression of science, whereas some of the main champions of Continental Philosophy have remained wholly sceptical towards the contribution of science to the progress of humankind. Thinkers beginning with Nietzsche and on to Heidegger, Albert Camus, Sartre, and the Frankfurt school, believed that the scientific and Enlightenment tradition bears some consonance with the legacy and continuance of European nihilism. Ameliorating this split is important for our understanding of the role of any radical atheism.

A more profound atheism will, I argue, offer a more universal and expansive sense of being human and allow humans to confront the question of nihilism circumventing the worst manifestations of the hollowing-out of civility and ethics. As mentioned, the scientific endeavour has, often quite unfairly, been seen as a handmaiden of nihilism. Disinterested knowledge reduces the world to a totality of truths; this world is comprehensible only in terms of wholly homogenous facts. Facts are neutral and can be returned to again and again, but neutrality in the fullest sense undermines any commitment to meaningful existence. These facts do not leave open, for example, the possibility of a determination of freedom, or a consideration of life and death. This is not to say that we should abjure facts, but that they should be seen within a lived and practical context. For this precise reason the famous lament of *The Gay Science* surpasses traditional atheism, in that truths are never truer than when they are lived or overcome.[3]

The atheism I will here propose takes the tradition of continental philosophy seriously. This is because it attempts to overcome the drive to nothingness and death which the mechanistic worldview of modern science has inaugurated. The point remains germane to this discussion. True atheism has to ground its actions in concrete and practical life and must be divorced from deathly mechanism, and the reduction of humans into brute objects of study. Nihilism, as defined by Nietzsche, indicates that our contemporary culture is suffering from an historical malady: the belief in nothing and the desire to perpetuate that nothing. This is axiomatic. The world is in a lot of trouble, engaging in seriously destructive tendencies. This is why Nietzsche – the thinker with whom we begin this book – of course is not an atheist, at least not in the conventional sense, and this radicalization of atheism is decisive for reconstructing any atheist or humanist endeavour. For Nietzsche, a committed scientific thinker such as Dawkins, or eliminative materialists such as Paul and Patricia Churchland, would be utterly symptomatic of the nihilistic illness: nature offers us nothing more than the sum total of material facts.

The drive towards materialism, towards an understanding of

the world in terms of matter, is a drive towards the inert, towards that which is without life and remains thus also a drive towards death: nothingness. But is it fair to suggest that science participates in this desire? Of course not: obviously, working scientists and individual researchers hold values, they understand what a mess the working production of real science can be. However, the point to keep in mind with Nietzsche is not so much to forsake the material world, but rather to resist our absorption into it. This is why Nietzsche's insight in *The Gay Science,* is about how one conceives of this collective endeavour in a way which has a stake in the present and future destiny of humanity and, put simply, in a way that is accessible to the lived world of human existence. It is not enough to say that it just does; the issue needs to be forced and this is where, and why, scientific atheism needs to be supplemented.

What resources of philosophical ideas can we draw on here to build the grammar of a radical atheism? Metaphysical atheism is, it must be noted, steeped in the drive to overcome nihilism. In order fully to understand this, we must understand the abstract idea of negation: we must understand it in roughly the context of what Heidegger called the nihilation of negation. In the most elementary terms, the question of temporality is decisive. If there is time, it follows there are events, happenings and becomings. Therefore, there is always occurrence, which ultimately negates the possibility of nothingness, since there must always be some event rather than nothing. Nothing is eternity, which must be the biggest zero of all as it is without occurrence or event. The essence of the human being, therefore, remains a curative, albeit a contested one, to the question of eternity and nihilism. Humans are essentially historical and self-determining beings, and the very brute fact of mortal life negates metaphysical nihilism. What atheism must definitively offer is the insight that the insidious nothingness that can seep into all aspects of human life, sometimes as the worst and most torturous burden, nonetheless can be overcome. Atheism must become a species of what Emmanuel Levinas would call first philosophy, where nothingness is negated, and all thoughts must begin with this insight. There is always something. If there is a human being in terms of its struggles in history, then the human being is defined by its action in addition to, and over and above, its physics. Thus Nietzsche's unsurpassable insight for how to overcome nihilism is that the human, because of its temporal nature in the face of the transience of reality, is itself the very possibility of overcoming nihilism.

Since transience and passing are such an essential part of mortal life, this fragility of life implies an exposure to violence, and it is, therefore, important to acknowledge and reflect on the violence of existence. In some sense, violence is integral to the cosmos. Humans can certainly have relative functions and purposes, but the cosmos itself is much more indifferent. To acknowledge the radical historicity of the human being is to envisage the human being eking out an existence in a turbulent and dangerous cosmos. Doing so entails that the majority of human actions are contested to begin with, but it is this very contestation which allows the human to engage in possibility, tragedy, universalism, truth, all in an effort to stave off the essential frailty of our species. Therefore, the human as species existing in, with and alongside a vibrant cosmos, has the capacity to transform and realize our nature for better or worse. In this book I attempt to offer a more radical account of atheism, where questions of things, time, truth, and universalism may be considered deepened for atheist discourse.

A radical form of atheism must be committed to the ubiquitous. It must look to the closest things beside it, as well as those at the farthest remove: the permanent questions of time, space and embodiment. It is absolutely necessary for the atheist to speak about violence and truth, finitude and life, and the shared and common life of our species. These are all themes which I examine in this work. Existential life necessitates the atheist's commitment to fragile procedures, being perpetually confronted with the all and nothing, the general and the particular, the universal and the specific. For the radical atheist, the truth of our universal species is beyond ourselves. Truth is not a thing out there, it is not some 'thing' that can be picked up and fondled. Truth is the condition of the world as it happens. Truth comes from a different place than the fleshy brain of the human. Outside of thought, outside of the confines of whatever world we inhabit, all regions of reality meet the wild truth of reality.

Although currently out of vogue, the task is to make a case for existential atheism because it has deep and profound resources for overcoming scepticism, relativism and nihilism. The task here is not to be negative towards science, nor any other discipline of thought, but to articulate a new atheist position. Atheism, which has traditionally equated itself with scientific humanism and empiricism, will be given a more expansive remit in this book. While the tradition of Enlightenment progress must never be forsaken, it is much richer to conceive of these notions in an existential sense. The fleshy material base of our empirical life must be conceived as both action and truth. What is required for the radical atheist is an existential empiricism, in the fullest sense of the empirical as both a test and a trial. Thus as much as the scientist in the laboratory is an empiricist staking out new regions of reality, so is the amorous couple who transcend the confines of their reality, as are all the drunks who stagger home in a lightly mystified version of reality, as much as the cyclist hitting their limits on an unmercifully steep climb, and to the transformed soldier returning from war.

Chapter 1

Liberating Nietzsche

Friedrich Nietzsche offers an undeniable challenge for the atheist. His philosophical reflections present an enormous obstacle to atheist philosophy, and offer its greatest potential also. Nietzsche's most famous critique of Western metaphysics is a critique of modern science as much as anything. Atheism as a humanist endeavour, as merely a question of belief, is a key contributor to the demise of the modern world. A reclaimed atheism has to take place beyond this. This requires thinking what a more radical form of atheism might look like in a more concrete sense, in order to stake out its precise coordinates. This call in Nietzsche's thought has never been taken up by atheism in a sustained fashion. Nietzsche offers a philosophical critique of different kinds of materialism – economic, scientific and cultural – and their attendant consequences for the ethical status of human beings. Nietzsche's radical form of overcoming humanism offers concepts from which a renewed atheism can begin. These are evident in his understanding of the temporal human, the re-figuration of the body, and the affirmation of humanity in the cosmos.

It is unsurprising that Nietzsche is concerned with materialism and economic nihilism. The Germany of Nietzsche's time was one of a rampant generalized self-satisfaction, set against the backdrop of recurring economic recessions and banking crises. Otto von Bismarck's rule in the latter part of the nineteenth century was synonymous with uniting in concord the various sectional interests of German culture, popular with the working class and German nationalists, and combined with military success abroad. For Nietzsche, Germany was content and in smug accord yet blissfully unaware of the spiritual dangers of such material happiness; while Bismarck's idiosyncratic social capitalism was Nietzsche's target as much as socialism and democracy, the common denominator among these was the idea of 'homo economicus,' i.e. economic man: the idea that the human was reducible simply to numerical or monetary terms.

Why is Nietzsche important for the atheist? It is because his critique of different types of economic and rational materialism, and their attendant secular ethics, opens up the opportunity to see atheism in a renewed light. Nietzsche really offers one of the first authentic expressions of what atheism might be in human terms. The most important elements of these philosophical coordinates can be shown mainly in his response to economic nihilism. In his effort to overcome the dull nihilism of the economic he turns to the historical dimension of human existence, the radical sensibility of the body, and finally forces conventional atheism to confront the impasse of scientific materialism. This is the terrain on which a deepened atheism must be reclaimed. Indeed Nietzsche presents a powerful and searing critique of traditional forms of atheism. Of course, the mantle of the atheist is not something that sits at all easily upon Nietzsche as we will see, and this is why he must be taken seriously for any vigorous theory of atheism.

Of all the things of which Nietzsche is regularly accused – perspectivism, relativism, individualism, proto-fascism, anti-Semitism, being a Svengali of capitalism – atheism is not usually listed. Nietzsche's importance for a radicalization of atheism lies in the challenge to the atheist to overcome reductive materialism and a crudely rational mathematization of the human. Nietzsche's view of the human is one that is a mix of the heroic and the precarious, a view of the dignity of human fortitude in the face of suffering. Human reality is the site of both suffering and possibility, of historical fate and its overcoming, and the most pivotal insight, the simple beginning for atheist reflection is that the human cannot be determined as merely matter.

9

Truly understanding Nietzsche involves understanding his brutal mixture of the fearful and the heroic. Nietzsche himself was a sufferer, and his visions of philosophizing with the hammer and the will to power easily fell on this sick and weak man who wept in the street to see the flogging of a horse. Nietzsche represents both the pitiful and the defiant at once, and indeed the susceptibility of these features to their perversion. Outside of any questions of atheist concern, one ought to sympathise with Nietzsche, since to do so is to sympathise with our own condition. Nietzsche's physical and psychological infirmities correspond to the existential confines and possibilities of the human. Nietzsche presents us with a view of the human as a combination of frailty, mortality, the desire for overcoming, and joy and despair.

What the atheist can truly take from Nietzsche are his protests against the current human, the human who has no sense of history or of the future. The most diminished form of human life is the human who has no sense of history, no sense of her own temporal existence. This is indeed why one of Nietzsche's texts is called *Untimely Meditations*: it is a paean to thoughts that go against the grain of current fashions and trends. We must hear the word 'currency' as both a temporal designation and a monetary one. The current human is the human who revels in all the illusory and immediate happiness provided by economics. If the radical atheist is to take their atheism seriously, they have to come to terms with the temporal and historical structure of life. The human for Nietzsche cannot and must not be determined as a 'current' being. The human in this sense is deeply negated, devoted only to the now. This negation must itself be negated in order to rescue humans from the homogeneity of the present. In this way, acknowledging that the human is a temporal being and a mortal being, constituted through the congealing of its past, present and future, is the beginning of overcoming atheism in order to produce a more profound version of it.[4] Merely existing in the world sets limits on what the human has been in relation to what they can become; the human in its essence is energised with power and capacity while being fundamentally bridled by the limited and finite.

The current man is for Nietzsche compounded by the world of science, numbers, and rampant industry. The current human is the average human, the statistical being; the one-dimensional man, as Herbert Marcuse would later term it. The current human is the taciturn upholder of capitalism. Meaning and value are only devoted to the current, to currency, and what is of the now. Meaning and value are only meaningful insofar as they serve the general interests of trade, immoderation, excess and destruction. The current human is the human who has not overcome herself. There is no sense of care for history or the future. These are serious problems for the destiny of humanity and are never a guarantor of ethical flourishing. Nietzsche's great problem is thus cultural nihilism; nothing is more repugnant to Nietzsche than a systematically quantitative culture. A utilitarian like Jeremy Bentham extolling the greatest happiness of the greatest number was anathema.[5] Numbers do not offer humans full perspectives on what is of worth and meaning. The quantification of the human being is the scandal of Nietzsche's times, the negative consequences of which would reverberate across the ensuing century.

In Nietzsche's great essay, 'Schopenhauer as Educator,' he argues that the *laissez-faire* model of economic capitalism diminishes pedagogy. Education based on the brute quantification of humans instrumentalizes the significance of the human being by applying industrial and productive values to the imperative of self-development. This process only results in the rational and self-interested human. The wider aim of such a form of education is the production of cultural homogeneity, an empty collective of "current" humans.[6] These humans have been dehistoricized, or to put it another way they are only dedicated to the immediate gratification of the present or the now. Indeed, for Nietzsche, the happier a society, the more 'current' it is, meaning the more pessimistic we should become. This is the society of nihilism, devoted purely to immediate gratification and the self-satisfied perpetuity of an un-philosophical life, of a life without questions and problems and where humanity and what it can become is not at stake.

The atheist after Nietzsche must resist reduction to mere material being or countable empirical properties. The salvation for Nietzsche of the human being is both an embrace of our material being and a negation of it. The human very much has a material and embodied being, but it is a matter that is trans-formable in itself. Our lived and visceral embodiment is tied to action and becoming. Nietzsche's potential to liberate atheism is his philosophical reflection on the temporal history of life, its central impulse being liberation from the confines of its world. The temporal negation at the heart of the human reveals the imperative to be, to strive, and to become. Thus the atheist, after Nietzsche, is a very different type of atheist, one for whom the material and cosmological account of reality is not absolute. After Nietzsche, atheism means that the human is its own becoming; it is its own action. Theory and practice become one for Nietzsche. Acting and thinking are philosophical in themselves. To be wise is to be engaged and acting in the world in a practical way. Instead of understanding the human being in a passive sense, as a mere aggregate of properties, the challenge that Nietzsche now sets for the atheist is to understand the human in the true light of what it is; a needy, striving, sensuous, aspiring, power-laden being. Nietzsche's liberation is a liberation from a ghostly and inert material world. The human is not predetermined by matter, which is to say by virtue of what it is; rather the human is as it does. We must of course not disavow the importance of matter, but we must think of it in a much more active sense. By mere virtue of being human we transcend the matter that we irreducibly are. Matter, as body, truly becomes a more radicalized matter, as an engagement with life and world, consequently inserting the human into history.

The axiomatic beginning for a radical atheism is that we are becoming agents. The human is its material embodiment and the negation of that embodiment. It is its projects and its material manipulation of the matter around it. Humans transform our most profound selves in the very act of doing, living, practising and transforming the world around us. Hence the atheist after Nietzsche must conceptualize herself as the subject of an accepted fate and situation in the world, but happily not determined as a mere puppet of the currency and fads of the age. It is, therefore, the task of the atheist to listen to Nietzsche's lament for souls of generations to come; this is the society of willing slavishness to the moment, to self-interest, to the fads of the *zeitgeist*.

Nietzsche gives the atheist the radical direction that is not present in mere matter. Atheism can reveal its true destiny, the negation of the society of the self, the society of the subject, and the society of the perspective. Nietzsche is committed to truth, and above all to overcoming perspectival truth. This is the claim that reality is fractured into different and relative truths which undermine all unified and coherent meaning. In perspectives, truth becomes nothing except subjective truth, where by extension everyone has a claim to the true. Nietzsche's atheist vector is thus Platonic, at least in this instance, in its desire to overcome the world of self-satisfied subjective opinion. This nihilistic malaise must be overcome in order to understand the connection of the human to its world, to itself, its possibilities and the far-reaching historical nature essential to its life.

Conversely, perspectivism is very corrosive for the human reality.[7] A relativist or pluralist state of affairs of the world diminishes the vitality of human capacities. Epistemological nihilism is hence reflected in psychological nihilism. A relativist or pluralist view of the world gives the self an ever-increasing internalization of the external world; any possibility of direction and purpose becomes exhausted in the face of the perpetual dissatisfaction with a fractured outside world, in turn becoming a tortured inner drama. Psychological nihilism occurs when every possibility is foreclosed, when the power and strength of a resilient and coherent human action becomes lost. All becomes nothing when faced with such relativistic nihilism. The more fractured knowledge is, the more damaging it becomes for the possibility of ethical life. This points to the task of the radical atheist: nihilism has made psychological insecurity habitual and *de rigueur*. In such a state of *ressentiment* the human being has no capacity for liberation and remains absolutely determined as itself, and as that which can be nothing else.

The atheist, following Nietzsche, must realize the psychological danger of such a pluralist state of affairs. The epistemological nihilism of perspectivism unleashes the potential for nothing at a human's core, and this is the greatest danger for the human reality both individually and collectively. To determine the human being as having a brute essence is to commit to nihilism, since it presupposes that the human cannot become anything. This is to say that there are no possibilities that can allow one to transform one's nature, and thus oneself, for the better or for the worse. Nietzsche here is the most perverted of Platonists. We are nothing, but this is what we must overcome; the true world is the world of becoming, not of a core and essential Being, and there is no absolute nature to things. Such a human, the current human, is utterly unhistorical. Time is not part of its horizon, and again, the human is utterly current, only savouring its own destruction.

But what can the atheist do? What coordinates are in place to overcome the essential nothingness at the heart of the universe? To be an atheist, one must rid oneself of atheism. Nietzsche undermines the atheist as radically as any other idol. The atheist for Nietzsche, in her contemporary state, is nothing more than the drive to the inhuman. What has to be embraced is Nietzsche's negation of the nihilism at the core of the human being, because the overcoming of nihilism he offers can contribute to the construction of a radicalized form of atheism.

The human being is all too human, both powerful and frail at one and the same time. The radical atheist human must, therefore, remain committed to herself from a state of malaise and alienation, to overcoming her confinement by the negative forces of existence such as anxiety, fear, threat, desires and goals. Unfortunately, as we have seen, psychological nihilism is also a species of economic nihilism. With utility and the democratization of egoism we can witness the cheapening of the masses. In essence, Nietzsche offers us the most anti-romantic gesture: the liberation of the human from the romantic 'individual'. And following in Nietzsche's footsteps, atheism must be ruthlessly committed to combating the individual who luxuriates in the confines and extension of the self. Nietzsche fires the salvo for a worthwhile manifesto of atheism. The cheap atheist is the thinker of cheap scepticism, the romantic hero, the pop star, the ne'er-do-well of culture, the beautiful loser that aestheticizes suffering, those who embrace fashionable negativity where negativity is embraced without reason. The mental decadence of nihilism: "unlearns modesty and blows up its needs into cosmic and metaphysical values."[8] Nietzsche's anti-romantic thrust rails against suffering in all its obdurate and inevitable guises, but more than anything, against the idea that suffering redeems the individual from the contingencies of the world. Nietzsche's famous radical human, the Overhuman, is thus, the human who liberates herself from her own internalization, who overcomes the confines of the ego and remains committed to her own outwardness: the Overhumans, alternatively, are humans open to the ethical possibilities of the universe, and participating in the universal events of the cosmos.

Any atheism worthy of the name must take Nietzsche seriously in his description of the cold justice of the universe. The universe does not guarantee anyone the good company of their own narcissism. Speculation on the justice of the cosmos is thus to be loved and feared. The value to the atheist in making humans more than just human, or simply determined humans, is the universe's cosmic indifference to human egotism. It is difficult to feel special once you realize the universe cares not a jot for your travails. Having a sense of this enormity is a curative to any atheist's delusions of grandeur, and reveals the visceral suffering humans attempt to overcome. Against such a backdrop, the human being must strive to free herself from all that is seductive and soporific. If we grasp that the world is absurd, if we truly realize that there is no ground beneath our feet, then this is truly liberating.

The atheist liberated must remain vigilant against the "…ways of self-narcotization."[9] This is the emptiness and void we attempt to fill with the current, with the now, with the un-temporal currency of immediate gratification in sex, violence, illusion, and hubristic science. To be human is to *be* a discourse on the visceral, on the idea that as humans, as much as anything else we are embodied, practical and acting beings. Such a reflection is something markedly missing in much traditional humanist and atheist discourse. Nietzsche's philosophy offers the question of the body to the radical atheist. The key point from which the atheist must not retire is the body as a site of suffering and tragedy that the human is impelled to overcome. Indeed this is what makes us most human, and any wish to turn one's suffering into a virtue is a form of self-abnegation. Nietzsche teaches the atheist to think of the body as active and lived rather than inert and passive. The body for Nietzsche is not a mere dead object of scientific study. We cannot understand the lived body in this way. The denial of the human body and its essential endurance is the denial of the activity of life; it is the denial of possibility, of what we can become. In turning the body into that which is current, the body becomes a machine. Why? Because here the body is nothing more than an object: it is reified, merely turned into a thing. This is why Nietzsche is essential for the radical atheist, who must guard against the lesser traits of scientific 'reductionism.' The body is always viscerally involved with the world, ecstatic in that which it is involved. In opposition, the inert body is nothing more than the working out of a mechanical programme where the body can be characterized as "...absolute obedience, machine-like activity, avoidance of people and things that would demand instant decisions and actions."[10]

But what of the body? What is it like and what does it offer to the atheist for ethical reflection? Firstly, the body is the most intimate commonality the human has with the world around it and the cosmos at large. The body is both a product of chance and an effort to stabilize the chaos it faces, and thus shares in the justice of the universe. As Pierre Klossowski notes, the body is "...nothing but the locus where a group of individuated impulses confront each other so as to produce this interval that constitutes a *human life*, impulses whose sole ambition is to de-individuate themselves."[11] Klossowski's point iterates our argument thus far. The Nietzschean project is an attempt to undermine the ego. Consciousness seduces us and attempts to negate the reality of the human being. It is so easy to forget our bodies, we forget they are there, simply because they remind us of the fragile reality in which we truly are and in which we participate. This is to say that awareness of our bodies in the world makes us realize that we are needy, vulnerable and violated beings.

Consciousness only grasps the body in the sense that it does not wish to come to terms with such a fortuitous nature. The site of our utmost fear is the place where we are most comfortable and which we find most easy. Yet there it is, sustaining us, nourishing and poisoning us, and allowing us to overcome the mere aggregate of impulses whence we always begin. The body, as Klossowksi puts it, is no longer synonymous with itself, it is not determined as a mere thing, it is not an instrument of consciousness.[12] The body is not there as a mere item that can be dispensed. Instead, it is fully active in adapting us to the world around us. The body is the locus of our sensibility to the world, and opens on to the cosmos, to what is dynamically happening all around us, and is thus wholly constructive in allowing the body to retain its relative stability in the flux of existence.

Klossowski's Nietzsche shows the body's ability to stabilize the impulses and forces to which humans react. In this sense the body mirrors the world around it, adapting and reacting, overcoming and being mutually influenced by it. What we are is the imposition of a flawed will on the emergence of the world and all its contingencies. The body is the site that ties Nietzsche's various concerns together. The body is the vulnerable body, it is the temporal body and it is the historical body. These questions are not part of the remit of conventional atheism, and they need to be answered to be meaningful in any way. The discourse of atheism must transfigure itself to deal with this-worldly affairs. Affairs of the lived body, the human enmeshed in its history, its temporal being and its desire to overcome suffering, all should impose questions on atheists for helping humans to understand their active part in transforming the confines of everyday life.

The point of returning atheism to Nietzsche, in order to move it forward, is to bring about a vigorous sense of the tragic thrust of human life. It is essential to do this, to overcome the indifference to the contingency of human events, to indulge in curiosity, and to temper the futural with a realistic dose of pessimism. This pessimism need not be debilitating, but can be one that opens us to the fragile possibility of human justice in the face of the brutal injustice of reality. The inconsequentiality of contemporary forms of atheism, its utter social and cultural vacuity in the face of real economic and political problems, needs to be overturned. Nietzsche is the first point where this can begin, he is not the last, but there is no better thinker for helping us to come to terms with the real suffering that is the inalienable skin of existence. Nietzsche challenges atheism to think the human beyond that which it can be and by that which it is relentlessly and sometimes fatally determined.

While it is impossible to say Nietzsche is an out-and-out atheist, at least not in the sense that your average humanist might define him, he nonetheless presents a visceral reminder of a world of possibility, the negation of the nothingness at the core of human existence, the overcoming of mandarins and gurus, a world where atheism in its most committed and sophisticated form can present a noble and vital body of thought which inspires a weighty and profound ethical alarm at suffering and human distress. With this in mind, Nietzsche places the onus on the atheist to develop the creativity, imagination, and empathy of the Overhuman. The common mistake that is made regarding the Overhuman is that it is founded on radical individualism or the idolization of a domineering authority. This is precisely what Nietzsche's philosophy opposes from beginning to end. The Overhuman is the human at the site of the historical destiny of humankind. It is a collective fate, where humanity's future, past and present condition is at stake. It is rare that you will find this sentiment in any form of contemporary atheism. Thus Nietzsche's aristocratic disdain for suffering and compassion is pivotal for challenging the valorisation of suffering, powerlessness, and the rotten malaise festering our futures and generating generations of bitterness.[13]

The collective destiny of humanity must be an issue for the reversal of values that Nietzsche seeks, which should be the Ground Zero of any passionate form of atheism. This is why Nietzsche is so interested in survival: because the fate of humanity stands on the precipice of its own destruction, not because he understood humans to be ruthless Darwinian avengers. The atheist has to become committed to understanding the temporal, the bodily and the utter necessity of overcoming the present. The atheist is strongest when she resists the absolute and totalizing rush towards the present, towards the eternal nothingness of the now. Such humans are those who realize the relentless justice of the universe, its utter fairness and the imposition of contingency on the human being, and humans who have proper pride in the collective destiny and accepted fate of humanity. Nietzsche was nothing short of an idealist in his rejection of romanticism.

Who will prove to be the strongest in the course of this? The most moderate; those who do not require any extreme articles of faith; those who concede but love a fair amount of accidents and nonsense; those who can think of man with a considerable reduction of his value without becoming small and weak on that account: those richest in health who are equal to most misfortunes and therefore not so afraid of misfortunes – human beings who are sure of their power and represent the attained strength of humanity with conscious pride.[14]

The atheist human is most human when mysterious and opaque, and when she is committed to interrogating her own condition and that of others. The Overhuman is the human without predication. We cannot say the human being is this or that 'thing' because it is spun out of its historical fate and futurity. To think of the future is not to think of ourselves, it is to think of the human outstretching itself towards all of the things which concern its condition.

To reiterate, the atheist, following Nietzsche, is a transitive being. The atheist human is not of the current, but is concerned with the ever-precarious lived and felt past, present and future. This is why the atheist must take up the baton of liberating Nietzsche. Human freedom, and the extent to which atheist freedom can coincide with it, can only begin to rediscover the importance of the central questions of a life which survives and a life worth living as a human. Nietzsche's nonchalant dismissal of the idols of his time is serious insofar as they are those who only see the future as a form of self-preservation. These types of people are the proprietors of time, existing as if owners of the past, present and future. The Overhuman is merely the human who accepts the inability to master time, and nowhere will you see the riches of this insight examined in contemporary atheism.

Atheism, if it is to be anything, has to share Nietzsche's alarm at the moral barbarity of the times, and the danger of losing ourselves to the forces of determination and currency. Atheism, if it is not committed to the collective activity and interests of humans, is literally nothing. The atheist must understand the bodily and disorienting harlequin effect that Nietzsche gifts to us in his philosophy, where the values of the weak become strong and those of the strong become weak. Here, embodied humans hold the future, past and present as collectively palpable. Atheism should always acknowledge the corruption of its age, of politics, institutions, and the psychological horror that is sensed at all times in human experience.

Chapter 2

Transparent Things

Transparent things, through which the past shines.[15]
Vladimir Nabokov

For thought, things are dark mysterious continents that are opaque to our cognitive colonisation as much as they are just what they appear to us. That humans are immediately enmeshed in things implies that our most immediate companions to any lonely thought are treacherous things. What does this have to do with the atheist? Lived atheism implies fascination with the things of this world. Atheism is existential in its obsession with the things alongside which it is situated. It must be, as these are a primary fascination: the sheer wonder that things just are the way they are, the fact that they are fragile and might possibly break or be moved, that they are arranged in such-and-such a way whilst also holding a cavernous enthralment. If walls could speak, how might they shame us; if walls could speak how might they save us? A radical atheism must be irrevocably intrigued by the perpetual fragility of things and what they might bring into being. The atheist's wonderment is inaugurated by the annihilation and obliteration of things which always accompanies the spaces we inhabit.

The things and objects of this world are radically divided. They can glimmer and seduce, or they can remain murky and mocking counterfeits of what we are. Things are transparent, holding a ghostly presence. Each individual thing is like peering over the edge of a door hinge into another room. From the limited panorama of the hinge, there is an immense and intimate vista opened up – immense in the radical depths which remain beneath the surface of how things appear to us, and intimate in the ever-ready proximity and security they promise. Things have their own history, inaccessible to us and beyond representation, and things are the most obvious elements of our immediate surroundings. They may be seductive and safe as well as dangerous and vicious, invested with grandiose symbolism as much as they can remind us of the mourning and loss which interlaces with our lives. Things, physical things, fabricated things, organic things, present themselves to us as dumbstruck and inert. They can absorb our attention as well as often meriting our unreserved indifference.

We handle things carelessly and sometimes with great scruple, but the inner structure of their world is as difficult to fix as ours. The great misconception of how things present themselves to us is that they are dumb, just there, without history. As the shell is presented to human perception it is presented as dumb, we perceive it as ignorant, just as it is itself, with very little relation to its immediate environment or the cosmos at large. We see a shell on the beach without thinking of the innumerable waves that have relentlessly crashed upon it, of the multitude of animals, humans and grains of sand which have passed over it through the duration of incalculable months, seasons and years. The shell as it is in itself holds a very flimsy veneer of reality. The most expansive reflection begins when a modicum shift in our thought process penetrates the slim film tension of reality which surrounds the object. Heidegger, in his tool analysis, is one of the key philosophers to address the unfathomable reservoir of reality in things. When we break through this thin filmic glaze that seduces us into the immediate world of objects, we can hear the sound of the sea deep within the shell: moreover, we can consider it being used as a tool such as an ashtray or an ornament, and we can picture it on a table face-up, receiving little wisps of ash. Atheist reflection begins when we recognize the presence that presents itself to us as utterly clear and decisive, but at one and the same time utterly nameless: the smile elicited by the shell as all the pain human drama can congregate.

Things present themselves to the human being as cracks in the very fabric of reality. Kant and Plato knew this well. Things give themselves as they appear to our experience. There is this phone, there is that ring, there are those books, there is that gun and as Edmund Husserl put it, they present themselves as they are with an honesty and integrity that convinces us of their absolute self-evidence. However, if we think the basic stuff of things we can see is that then they are never merely just what they present themselves to be. They are always other to themselves. At the heart of a thing is an indication of the cosmos beyond, if only indirectly. Atheist reflection must begin with what is before its eyes as part of the wider environment. By simply reflecting on things in our immediate experience, we know that they are never just the gossamer film of their appearance. They are always more than their profile, their material. Things, whether we know it or not and irrespective of the fact that they do not know it, have their own history, and their own interior. They are there not because they just are themselves in themselves, but because they are positioned in relation to other things. They are what they are not. Things are thus spectral for humans. They are always there yet easily forgotten. They are of momentous political and literary significance and stand in opposition to human activity in life. They are there, in pure opposition as spectral appearances, and it is here that the human becomes the accused. What is pivotal is that the democracy of things alongside our existence clamours for attention, and makes reflexive for the human our factuality and lived context. They insert the question of existence at the core of the human. They burden the human with the questions: "why are you not me," "why are you not this chair," "what can you do not to be us?" They are the most dangerous site of seduction, enticing the human to become absorbed in the populace of things. The human exists alongside a multiplicity of things which present the easy task of existing alongside them in their mute forgiveness. We can so easily become the things of our own world.

For the atheist, things tell us something about truth. This is because they are constantly dying. Things, truth and death are decisively entwined. This is one of Plato's great insights, and one that is essential to understand for the birth of atheist reflection. For Plato, the truth of life was essentially related to death. Living in this world was no more than a primitive shadow of the truth, akin to dwelling in a perpetual effort to pass a second-rate course in seduction. The things of this world are in effect the speed-dating version of a loving relation with the truth. For Plato, living was ephemeral and passing, while death was on the side of the immutable. Since truth must remain steadfast and constant it thus also bears a spectral companionship with death, and is also, therefore, on the side of the immutable. Death is, therefore, the all-consuming twilight of all things. Therefore, the things of this world are nothing more than lustrous stars, as alluring as the latest Hollywood fad. The sad truth of mortal life is that it is ever-changing and temporal, swaying the human from one thing to another. However, death in the Platonic sense is the true realm of that of which we can be certain. Plato's great insight for the atheist is that death thus has an erotic relationship with truth.[16] Things always have their beyond; that which is most intimate with things is their own mortality. It is for this reason that things can open up to us that which is of the greatest significance. The death of the life of things opens up the whole domain of existence in all its nuance and possibility. To know, to love deeply and truly, is at one and the same time a reflection on how the things closest to us are embroiled in death. But this is the essential revelation. They reveal that death and nothingness lie at the heart of existence and that this is the truth of things.

Plato, however, only carries us so far. The death of things reveals that a mute and infinite silence resides behind all objects.

Atheist thought must treat this silence as any other thing, with a death of its own. The common dissolution of all things is seductive as it is the common denominator that hides behind all things, promising an unfettering from the ghostly shackles of things. This thought extends to all of reality. As humans are positioned in opposition to the world, behind all things dwells the possibility of nothingness. It is as Maurice Blanchot thought, the momentous moment when all different things, all different events contain their own negation.[17] This is the beginning of everyday life, the hither and thither of thoughts, organization and relationships. What Blanchot notes, following Emmanuel Levinas, is that all the things in existence have in common is the potentiality of their own negation: birds, chickens, deer, grains of sand, nebulae, solar storms all come to an end. The panorama which Blanchot opens at all points in the universe after all things are dissolved is a blank and infinite nothingness. That which binds all is a mute silence: infinite, cold and austere. It is a silence that transcends all things. By virtue of its expanse it is never localised to particular things or spaces. It has no empirical content and remains as intransigent and stubborn as male machismo. It is the slime of the cosmos, the absolute negation of all birth and creation that sticks to all things. Why is this infinite silence dangerous? Because it is an absolute death, it is absolute nothingness, cold, serene and eternal. Eternal life is nihilism. It is the thought that no-thing can happen; it is, therefore, in essence the most pristine expression of nihilism. It is inhuman and the cosmic engine behind all negation, bringing all things to a stop in a recalcitrant duration. It is the power of nothing.

For atheist thought, and indeed as we will see for Maurice Blanchot, this negation must be negated; the human being is the exceptional counterpoint to this silent executioner.[18] Things are important for atheism because they reveal the limits of negation. Bodies emerge, objects form, life passes. The human being is certainly a thing of this world, and a body amidst things. What separates it from other things is that it realizes it shares in the destiny of all of the objects in the world. In addition, the human holds the recognition of its potential objectification and its resistance to a reduction to things. Why does the human have this exceptional quality? It is because it has the capacity to transform the nothingness behind all objects into something. All objects can be otherwise; the human as an object, even if it shares the destiny of many things in the universe, can have a relation to the possibility of its own negation. It can reflect deeply enough on the expansive sense of things, their history and possibility, whilst sharing in the common destiny of all things that exist. Atheist thought, therefore, emerges every time humans begin to act, to do, to engage and to relate to others. What defines atheist thought is that it is always the inauguration of a beginning. The very presence of beginnings is the ever-present negation of absolute nothingness. Indeed, humans in all their singular instances, at innumerable points in time and space, are the collective negations of nothingness. Meditation on the things of this world is important for atheism because these reflections reveal, embedded in the human, a call to remain sensitive to the fragile significance and collective state of all humans.

Whether such a call is answered is another matter entirely. But things in themselves insert the possibility of resisting absolute negation in all its instances at the heart of the human being. What characterises the atheist most definitively is thinking the human as sensitive to the beginning of creation.[19] The task of atheist thought is to think with creativity, imagination and sensitivity to the vista opened in the face of absolute negation. The bearing of atheist reflection is at once sustained through the negation of the nothingness that exists at the heart of all things. Thus what defines the atheist most of all is the existential reality that birth is always close to the things of this world. At the core of things is the negation of absolute nothingness. This is a tentative and fragile thought, precarious in its appreciation of the nature of all reality. Certainly, as Heidegger thought, what distinguishes human life from animal or inanimate life is that the truth of all we say and do comes to fruition in death. This is an important moment for atheist thought. Certainly, the human is born in the sweat or violence or the awkward kindness of sexual encounters and ends in the putrid decomposition of the grave, but this is not all. In the hither and thither of living, that which is most significant is that the human begins in the face of the placid inertness of things. Essential to atheist thought is the most pressing and urgent matter of the things which open up the spaces in which things can be organized, wherein they can be given bodily life, where new arrangements can be made.

The visionscape of atheist imagination is always a matter of imagining beginnings as much as it is one of endings. It is the question of organizing our beginnings and endings throughout life in an effort to negate the absolute nothingness which, without vigilance, lays claim to all regions of the universe. Since things essentially hold the capacity to dissolve this, they are transformative and remind of us of the potential to begin new situations. For the radical atheist, this provides ontological proof of the persistence of re-emergence and regeneration at the core of human reality. Since there are events, and things in themselves are events, it follows that the nothingness of absolute and eternal peace cannot be resident. It only exists as a result of the glimmering spectral shadows which are the superficial sheen of things. While things are a liberation, they are thus also a seduction. Things and what they promise are the first step for the atheist in necessarily overcoming the anonymous slime of eternal nothingness that sticks to all things. The essential and transformative fact with which a more profound atheism begins, is that life is not reducible to the worst. Indeed, this is the actuality of human living for atheist life. Death is not the only phenomenon in life, and no matter how malevolent the violent vicissitudes of life, it is always possible to liberate oneself from the cycle of things and begin again. If this were not the case, human existence would no longer be an issue since it would become a thing to such an extent that it would be utterly objectified, and absolutely reified as a thing to such a degree that all humanity would be evacuated from it.

The burden this places on the human is the task of negating the thingliness of human existence. While the human lives in a world of spectral things – here, there, over there, always accompanying us – what these things reveal is the opening of the human being into a living and existing in the world. A reflection on things, their banality and singularity, mitigates against the human being becoming reduced to things, but also, in a connected way, mitigates against the loneliness of the sovereign subject. Atheist thought must exhort human beings to remain sensitive and imaginatively open to the history of things, to the history of contact with other human beings and, indeed, to other beings. Admittedly there are instances where things are a burden, like stacked shelves of pale and rose-cheeked grimacing dolls, but there are always other things that negate our immediate environment. The atheist who is committed to negating nothingness in all its forms must resist the human being's active absorption into the world of things. The objectified human being, as much as the human who becomes immobilized by obsession or the fetishization of things, is alienated from the world as much as the world of possibility. The things which face us, exhort us and accuse us, immediately, in all their multiplicity, resist the ideal of mastery which is dogging so much thought in philosophy. The thought that we can ground the human being in a self, free from self-alienation, only results in a philosophy grounded on its own self-contained and self-generating power of reflection; here the world of things is nothing other than a reflection of the subject herself, which is about as useful as a sports commentator commenting on her own contribution to the sport upon which she commentates. The world of things strikes an enigmatic note within the world of human possibility, presenting both danger and liberation. Things are the objects of the world, nature, imagination, art, and the activity of history itself. They are also the world which can absorb humans with the dream that we can manipulate them willy-nilly. Things are not something we can wholly master, but they do exhort a strange power over us, a power for liberation or seduction.

Crucially, combating nothingness is integral to atheists' lived experience and essential to the atheist's ways of life in order to overcome nihilism. In all things, relations and social organizations, there is the possibility of negation. At the core of human experience there is always this possibility. Things, ideas and people come and go, whereas the possibility of destruction remains forever. The atheist lives in opposition to this corrosive reality, indeed the atheist has no choice but to live in opposition to this experience and try to impose order and purpose on it. Why? Human existence is always a coming into existence. The human is always facing new events and new things. The things of this world hold their own contingency; things are alert, vivacious with the potentiality of their own negation. A human life is determined to an extent by these things. My immediate environment as I run, sit, go about my business, ponder, or worry about taking a payday loan, is entirely made up of things which can disappear. There, right at the core of my existence, is the possibility of slimy destruction. They determine my lived environment, indeed I exist among them insofar as I am a thing among them which also dissolves.

If the question of the void haunts and mocks us at all times, then it is one that also opens us outwards. How does such horizontal transcendence happen? It occurs in the sense that we are our world, that we are things that move beyond the cellular meanderings of our own imagination. All the things that we encounter or of which we can think negate ourselves. As Jean-

Paul Sartre well knew, things assert a dizzying liberation at the heart of existence: the transcendence of the ego directs the human outwards. For the atheist, this onerous freedom gives the human an essential task. Human existence is always a negation of nihilism. This is decisive. Human existence has the possibility of liberation *tout court*. To resort to nothingness is a privation of the creation of beginnings. The sheer abyssal and precarious fact that the human being exists, as it does, amidst things, burdens us with the insatiable urge to overcome our reduction to things. I am chosen by things insofar as I am not them. This means that one of the most essential human experiences is that what I am is what I am not.[20] For the atheist, then, the most essential question that is posed for our existence is one of resistance. It is resistance to being reduced to things. It is resistance to seduction by things and it is resistance to the objectification of the human.

Insofar as we are determined, radical atheism is determined by overcoming the objectification of the human. What I am, what I can be, what I was, indeed the whole of my life is liberated because it negates nothingness and nihilism. All of my life is thus determined by things, insofar as I am one of them. All my life is also determined by not being these things: atheism instantiates within the human the unquenchable demand upon humans to liberate themselves from these things which they are not.

The question of things also brings into relief the question of time. Insofar as lives are determined by things as channels for our hopes, ideals, and political and social relations, they also insert within us the notion that we are not yet. Things impose on us their utter contingency. All of my living between birth and death is never anything absolutely determined. Things thus take up a temporal understanding since they impose on the human the question of the past and the future. The contingency of things installs contingency at heart of existence and everything which contingency implies: lack of control, anxiety, comedy, farce and insecurity. Things, both real and imaginary, populate our thoughts with anguish and flourishing. That I am here implies that things have a say in the organization of my past, present and future. That I will be there cannot be thought of without things.

Things, and the possibility that I will merely become one, stridently announce the essential insecurity of being human. They are the limits and borders of mortal life, staking a claim to who I can become and directing what fate has in mind for me. The contingency of things relates me to the totality of existence. Their contingency installs within me the question of existence. Transparent things imply that existence is always in question. They remind one that it is only by virtue of surpassing my reduction to things that I am able to relate to my own existence, the existence of others and existence as a whole. The immediate and mundane experience of things given in my world then reminds me that I am not reducible to things. For the atheist, the human being cannot be a thing or a mere aggregate of properties but must be, more decisively, the surpassing of the possibility of becoming a mere thing among others. The atheist's essential emancipatory thought is that the transparency of things is never just the object that they present themselves, and neither is the human who experiences them.

Things remind us of the totality of things constantly. Every single thing, whether a pebble or a pencil, indicates beyond its immediate presentation to our experience: each thing imposes on us the sheer question of the contingency of all things which have existence. All things can be otherwise and therefore the human being is stripped of luxuriating in its immediate environment. Things inhabit the present but do not dwell there. The human dwells with them, but upon self-reflection she realizes her palpable contingency and is opened to the future. The temporal texture of things corresponds to Heidegger's idea of temporality. Things oblige us to negate the present, or the world of the brute presentation of information from the senses. For the radical atheist, that things do this has an important consequence. The question of liberation is always at hand. We certainly may be reduced to 'just the way things are' – in innumerable contexts from the torture chamber, to the sexual abuse victim, to a repetitive dreary job – but things can always be otherwise. Thus the key philosophical question is the atheistic question. How can I negate the nothingness at the heart of all things? To do this, I have to understand that the self is always a form of horizontal 'transcendence'. It is related to others, to ideas, to things, to political configurations as much as to works of arts. This is why things are important for humans. They negate the self, taking the human out of their ego. But this is also why they only serve a limited use: the temptation to become absorbed with things is a temptation as old as the myth of Midas. But things do reveal something. I am always more than the now, than the things which populate my experience. This is because I am a temporal being. As Nietzsche judges becoming, what characterizes human existence more than anything is that the questions of past, present and future have a palpable and intense span. For humans, their relations and the events which constitute their life are never the present world of things around them. Hence, for the human being and their friends, the past is never a thing and neither is the future. Unlike the lamp next to me, the past is never only the past, and neither is the future only the future. Instead, they are integral parts of the lived factuality of existence.

Crucially, the human being is not *absolutely* determined by transparent things. Were the human being only one of these things it would be enveloped in a world without possibility. In short, we could never be otherwise than what we are. That things always hold this dark, shimmering negation offers us a dark liberation. We *are* insofar as we inhabit a world of things, but we *are not* insofar as things cannot determine our selves absolutely. This difficult freedom inserts an eviscerating question at our core. It is the question that we are; an unquenchable question which governs all systematic struggles to come to terms with the transparency of things. It is the question of how to overcome the negation to which all things are beholden.

How does my life become more than the things that I am? How do I become a being which is more significant than the mere shining or darkness that things can evoke for us? For the atheist, the contingency of all things is the momentous question that accompanies all humans. Since we are limited by all the things in our proximate environment, we are in a strange way tied to the destiny of those things. Since they are always open to destruction then I am not these things. The kernel of the argument is that the nothingness behind things is always negated. We are constantly seduced by things in our everyday life, either as commoditisation or just in dull unthinking experience. Philosophical reflection reveals the possibility and destiny of things, and how they are always tied up to the creation and formation of new bodies; that these things are premised on their own termination reveals for the atheist that the most essential thing that must be overcome is the absolute negation of all things. If the human is one among these things, and there is a deep void at her heart, this violently inserts in the human being a moment of transcendence. The human is a void, it is nothing in solidarity with things, but it is a nothing for which creation is always a question.[21] That the human is a thing is true, however insofar as it is not determined as a thing allows us to understand the question of beginning which is at the core of reclaiming atheism. Hence, reflecting on things reveals that for the atheist the most important question is how to overcome nothingness. What consumes the atheist, the atheist's passion, is thus overcoming the nihilistic possibility at the heart of all things.

Chapter 3

A Violent Truth

As the previous chapter has shown, the multitude before our eyes reveals much for atheist reflection; things reveal the possibility of the 'all'. They bring to light the question of truth. Things can be arranged in innumerable ways but are not infinite. This sets a limit on what we can know and thus raises the question of truth in the broadest possible sense. The importance of this for any atheist is that truth is not an object, but rather it is tied to the history of different events, occurrences and happenings. For the atheist, the human is thus one insofar as it is many. Atheism nourishes itself on the ineliminable mystification of humans living on the shores of existence. Every thought reveals the limitations of human action in relation to the totality of existence. Existence is there, haunting and accompanying every single thing we do. When we shop, travel on a bus, love, hate, existence is there. The most banal thing, whether it is soap or a sock, is at once mundane and utterly enigmatic. The speakers on the desk beside us always have an excess over how we directly perceive them. It is what it merely is, but it is also so much more. When we fold back the veil of sensory information, what is revealed is something more real than what we take for granted.

Such a world is violent; there is no peace found in this world of atoms, molecules and electrical forces. Everyday existence is utterly weird once we reflect upon it. Every single thing we perceive is an abyss of associations, antagonisms, connections and divergences. There, right behind what is before our eyes, is the torrent of all existence. Atheism illuminates this existence, one present alongside our everyday life. It is the multitudinous exchange of innumerable things that begs the question of truth. In a way, we co-exist with the things of our world, enmeshed in an indifferent reality. Radical atheism is thus a question of truth since the reality of what can only exist is imposed upon thought. The question of truth arises because the human is thus essentially limited, and can only think beyond itself with regard to the arrangement of reality. The human being must submit to the way things are. Thus the truth of reality is always there, demanding and forceful. This chapter will articulate the necessary imposition of truth upon humans by virtue of the vicissitudes of reality.

The question of radical atheism is always the question of expressing the human's place within the dynamic of the nature of reality itself. Most importantly, life begins with a negation of the human being's mundane reality. This is not to say that everyday life is secondary – it is rather to emphasise that it is drastically weird. I am Patrick and the collection of my historical experience and possibilities, and I participate in all of the atomic collisions and sub-atomic events that have happened to bring this singularity into being. I am certainly not extraordinary or a phenomenal being, but merely one among many; indeed, it is utterly fortuitous that I am here at all.

Every object which exists as we perceive, has at its core a sublime negation which reveals to the human being the possibilities of other beings. The more the human reflects on the wild multitude of reality, the more palpable a sense it has of the negation of all things. This is decisive: the more everyday life and the things of this world become other than themselves, the more we sense the contingency of the isolated objects around us which determine our situation. By extension, the negation of all the things in our situation hints at the flagrant negation at the core of all things. The sheer contingency of the world around us, its profiles and qualities entails that humans and the things of this world in our immediate situation are not absolutely determined. The appearance of this minimal negation at the core of all being illuminates starkly that the human situation amidst the things of this world is one which is potentially open to disintegration. The world as it is there before us presents itself as a unified field. All of the things which are present to us are there, cradled in a relative unity *as if* they were mutually connected. However, the more the human remains sensitive to this difficult truth of existence, the more she can realize the relations between the world as it appears and its violent and turbulent reality. The more we embrace the fact that the smug reality of sense perception is disintegrating, the more human we become, since the more we will have a sense of attunement between the proportion of our immediate situation and the eerie vistas of existence which lie alongside them.

The atheist is thus equipped with a humble sense that she can draw equivalence between any two objects. Anything which occurs can be put in contact with anything else. This of course can be attributed to the vicissitudes of the human imagination; however, there is something more at stake here. The human ability to cognize, to discern, judge, negate and draw similitude, illuminates the inescapable proximity of singular things and the total relation of things. That things exist, anywhere and everywhere, implies the startling and impossible isomorphism of thinking and reality. Even if we are limited by our cognitive abilities, or the aggregation of our sensory experiences, all of reality is always a question for us. We act out this desire every day within the confines of our everyday life and the world that surpasses that. We cope, desire, aspire to *be*, as well as to master the world. Insofar as the human being lives, thinks and reasons, it does so as it struggles against its limitations in coming to understand the truth of reality. Thus for the radical atheist, truth is an exercise in thinking the transgression of her everyday world with philosophical enquiry. Any being that exists may only be because it can be affected by other beings. The cosmos is violent, embroiled in turbulent energy, blasts of heat, light and cold, swirls of atomic collisions. From the miniscule to the enormous, reality is a welter of collisions, contaminations and penetrations.

This backdrop is the nexus between everyday reality and the cosmos. To say what an atheist is, is thus to place the atheist within the Greek tradition of situating the human between the earth and the sky. In my terms, however, the atheist occupies a space between the earth and the stars, becoming the fleshy embodiment of the space between the infinitely small and the infinitely large.

In a paradoxical sense, reality is the product of the necessity of contingency. The things which lie beside us, even at the corner of our eye, in the periphery of our vision, are subject to a dissembling, either infinitely small or infinitely large. If this were not so I would be no different to that chair, that table, that floor, that electronic gadget, and neither I nor these things could become anything else. That the empirical human is determined solely as a thing would undermine any possibility that one's existence could transform itself, that one could transform one's existence, or the world around us. This is, as Terry Eagleton often puts it, the dumbest type of empiricism, where all you see is what you get.

Atheist astonishment and wonderment begins by drawing a radical equivalency between the things of this world and the utterly astounding fact that all of reality is there at all, in all its concatenations and diversity. The human in the face of the flurry of events which surround it can be steadfast or fragile in its commitments and projects; however, as it struggles and aspires for its life to be the measure of reality, it is faced with a poignant negation. It cannot master all of its reality, let alone all of reality itself. That it cannot be reality is the ultimate negation of its efforts at mastery. The human being as it aspires to ascend to reality is thus in some sense tragically negated of this grasping by innumerable factors: by its death, by occurrences and events, by the minutiae of miniscule sub-atomic events, by the sheer proximity of transparent things, by the vanity and inauthenticity of its projects and by the dynamic structure of reality itself. In consequence the human being is essentially vulnerable, in that any aspiration it holds with regard to the summit, or the totality of things, is susceptible to its own negation. Atheism, inasmuch as it begins with astonishment at the sheer contingency of things, must also realize the limited possibilities that are imposed on our historicity. In this way only the atheist is truly philosophical, since she acknowledges that the human is an evolving and reflective mind within the wider cosmos in which it is entrenched. Atheism is thus a form of thinking that allows the human to engage, map and reflect the truth of the material world in all its vibrancy.

What more can we say is at the atheist's core? If the truth of the human is in sublime negations, then the atheist is the site of an existential violation. As George Bataille envisaged, reality itself coldly lacerates itself. Reality, in its entire swarming, crawling and creeping multitude, violently negates any primordial peace within the cosmos. For this reason any human engagement with the world, any human transformation of the material stuff that produces the world through labour or aspiration, is violated to a greater or lesser extent. For this reason, the atheist experience is the philosophical experience *par excellence*. Atheism is placed at the core of human reflection since its task is a reflection on the human being as the precarious site of the most human things of all: living, sharing, having a sense of the cosmos, and the organization of political communities. Mortal life becomes what it is, the realization of relative order in an indifferent cosmos.

Atheism from its inception demands a repeal of aggressive egoism. There is no necessary connection between the atheist and the most distant events of the universe. The universe after all does not care one iota for the human being. To pretend otherwise is nothing more than the mildest form of aggressive narcissism. All the mysticism that rigorous scientific experimentation attains about the immensity of the universe falls short in opposition to the infinite becoming and the violent impenetrable chasms which nonchalantly ebb and flow around our minute speck of a planet. To live atheism then, to live our most absolute human sense of vision and depth, we must struggle to resist the vain extensions and self-aggrandisements of human consciousness. The ever-present temptation for the human is to aspire to be reality, to aspire to make all the things of this world commensurate with all of reality itself. In opposition, the only pride the human can attain is an acceptance of its essential nature as a glittery and fortuitous piece of dust that shares its being with all the violent events of the universe. The human is a result of violence, and will pass out of, or even on to, reality wrenched of whatever it has called life.

All of this might imply that the atheist should not take pride in her place in the cosmos. As Ray Brassier puts it, human existence must realize it is of no intrinsic worth. Philosophy "should always be more than a sop to the pathetic twinge of human self-esteem."[22] There is something to be said for this idea that human vanity tends to place itself at the centre of the cosmos, and that philosophy should always attempt to divest itself of this temptation. Brassier is absolutely right to criticize the narcissism of human self-esteem in the name of an enlightened realism. However, human vanity is derived from experience, and the over-determination of our experience as universal. The truth of reality is never just what is simply experienced in the flux of life. Plato knew this well. More decisively put, for the atheist, truth is the recognition of reality as the state of things as they are at the intersection of how they are coming to be. For the atheist, human experience is thus always dependent on what radically exceeds experience. The human relationship with truth is thus always in some way related to death and violation. As it should be for the atheist, the conditions of finite life are always the point where the illuminations of truth and how they connect with the turbulent world of reality can begin to take flight.

An important departure from Brassier is that there is a difference between the notion that all reality and knowledge is derived from the human, and the idea that human existence is a being amongst things in the world. The idea that the human is but a mere symptom of reality, that it is emergent out of disorder, implies that it is not the original passive receptacle of all that exists. The atheist knows that the human is not the truth of reality nor, more importantly, has she privileged access to such truth; the human does not live *in* the truth, nor is truth a mere thing of the world around us. Truth relates to the human when we realize the necessities imposed upon us by reality. Truth is the realization of the logical limits that existence imposes upon humans. This is the very reason of the world and reality.

Atheism must thus always reflect on why things are thus and why they can only be thus. Why does the atheist know this more than anything else? Because the atheist is subject to the lacerations of reality; the very negations of existence impress upon the atheist the relentless tension between the felt durability of things and the world at hand, and the incessant becomings to which these things are subject. This is the beginning of judgement and reason. Indeed, the atheist stands between the relative durability of all things and the possibility of their radical contingency. To know is to engage and do, and to make knowledge possible insofar as we can assert the truth of that which happens. Truth is, therefore, what cannot but happen.

Atheist illumination is a fragile truth. Truth is never a question of the human becoming reality; it is a reasonable reflection on the reasons for existence, emerging as it does within the dimensions of its shapes, structures and forms. The marvellous fact that reality is organized simply thus, demands a reflection on why it is there and how it coheres as it does in the face of the violent events comprising it.

If the atheist stands somewhere between the earth and the stars, the starry view to which she is privy is an absolute vista of the utter precariousness of the things of this world as well as their gentle permanence, and their irretrievable organization. This intimate relationship between truth and death provides the atheist with an essential illumination. Truth is procreative. The things of this world may only be known in the course of a life; reality itself generates innumerable events and states of affairs. As Blaise Pascal knew, the miniscule span of a human life, before and after its lived temporal span, is directly engulfed by an absolute immensity of unknowable spaces.[23] Pascal's fear of course is that these unknowable spaces comprise pure unadulterated nothingness. This is also a concern for the radical atheist, but one that is logically undermined by the transformative structure of reality. Nothingness is impossible *tout court*. This is because the contingency of things happens. Any event is the negation of nothingness. If the atheist begins reflection on the ubiquity of laceration and violation, then her most immediate question is always the birth or bringing into being of the negation of nothingness. Traditionally in philosophy, that which is beyond life and human cognition is the realm of death, but here it is also the realm of becoming and generation, of the making of things as they are. This is hugely important for the atheist: that truth is procreative sees the human as essentially violated and a struggle, but a violation that opens the human to the relation between what it is and what is out there, between its flesh and body and the beyond. Existence, therefore, imposes on the human the unquenchable urge to know why things are born as they are. Thus the pivotal point is that the violent truth of reality is always of the utmost importance for any atheist.

The radical atheist is impelled to understand the tension between an unremitting desire to cling to life, and the truth that such reality is born from the death pangs of cosmic life. The visceral experience of atheism is the birth, death and the yearning to know; atheism is truly the most philosophical experience in that its desire to know propels it beyond the mere everyday things of lived experience. This concoction of birth, death and love is an illumination in itself, opening the human both to brute immediacy and to the impossible distance of all that is. Beset by the violent truth of the glistening transience of reality, atheism demands the discovery of the macrosphere and the microsphere and how things come to be; that the world is thus, and has come to be in no other way and yet remains bizarrely other.

All events in the cosmos will be born and die in such a way that there is structure and dissolution, entropy and evolution in the macrosphere, whether the environment and its laws affect me, or whether they are the chimeras of the fleshy lump of ganglions I call my brain. Philosophical atheism as desire is thus always a meditation on love; between birth and death, the atheist is beset with the desire to understand the spooky generosity which means that things are thus, and exist as they are. The sheer fact that the cosmos allows things to exist means atheist reflection is grounded in relation to a terrible love for the flimsy things of this world with which we are enmeshed. The radical atheist is beset with a desire to know why reality comes to be as such, not only human reality but the reality of the history of the universe and its fate.

The question of history is always important for the atheist in negotiating the miniscule and the colossal. The atheist at her core is simply the being who is perplexed and enamoured with the nature of temporality, of space and of causation. The atheist is driven by a love of becoming, and it is this love that illuminates and reveals one's mortal life in terms of a radical history, both human and cosmic, terrestrial and stellar, reasonable and irrational. The atheist is the locus of the central philosophical question, 'why is there something rather than nothing?' along with a more profound adaptation. This question of existence must also be the question of what magnitude this fleshy embodiment may have in the terms of the vast extended expanse of reality.

Existence is a violent laceration; thought begins with the permeation of life with death. Reality illuminates the atheist; it whips and snaps her into cold vision. Atheist thought proceeds with the sound of a whip cracking; a severe and sharp wound followed by a speculative release onto the vista of all of the events that are occurring in reality. Indeed, this is why philosophy is the most atheist thing of all. The central question that the atheists face is why does this not make sense? But at one and the same time how marvellous it is that it does not, and astonishing that all of these things for no apparent reason unintelligently form. The universe imposes this question on us, and thinking is shot through with an imperative to answer it. It is this question which is the engine of our philosophical and scientific explorations. In this sense, atheism is the wedding of metaphysical astonishment and scientific discovery, wonderfully populated by the terrestrial and the psychological, the solar and the cosmic and the manner in which these are thrown together in the broadest possible sense. While the expanse of reality may be far beyond the cognitive scope of both human imagination and tactile extension, nevertheless the turbulent nature of reality inserts the philosophical question of atheist existence at the core of mortal life. Reality demands that the human grasps reality in its terrestrial, stellar and cosmological entirety. As we live, this drives the most pressing human questions, which is to say what are the most immediate forces governing one's existence.

Once philosophy realizes its atheist destination, human liberation is possible. The radical atheist can, as Hamlet intimated, accept the slings and arrows of outrageous fortune. In the gloomy and mysterious darkness of the universe the atheist might be tempted to see her sanity with some gravitas, as the haughty grasping of a candle flame in the face of the invading squalls of absurdity. This however is dangerous and closes down thought, as this is the person that can turn the cold indifference of reality into something cheaply defiant. While the cynical nihilist delights in her ability to turn all aspects of reality into nothing, this ultimately is the last bastion of narcissism. I cannot commit because I know the way the world is. I know reality is contingent and therefore I have a privileged access to a Faustian truth. I know reality is nothing more than the concatenations of movement, changes and the most radical form of contingent negations. Solipsism and relativism are the delusions of the most negative form of cynicism. The cynical nihilist stands fraily defiant as the last impediment to thinking the core of the human being. The liberation that atheist illumination brings to overcome this posturing, is that the turbulent reality of violence imposes the inescapable possibility of truth, sensitivity, freedom and action upon the atheist; that is the sensitivity to the universe in all its 'machinations', the freedom to overcome one's historical conditions and the actions which sustain them; as Nietzsche knew, in a reality of eternal becoming, what comes to matter is what exists and is done rather than what is not done.

Radical atheism is, therefore, not a paean to protean change, only to change insofar as it has an impact on what exists. Atheist reflection thus always has a certain errancy to it. It strives to match the violent punctuations to which innumerable groups, peoples and objects subject human existence. Its resilient core is strangely perennial; its concern is the human recognition of the tremors of reality that perforate all local identities and their common reality. It owns no truth, it has no propriety or territory over whatever authority bequeaths as truth. Atheism strives to discern the reality of what is happening in the present alongside the vectors of what has been and what will come to be, setting itself the task of illuminating what is singularly historical with that which is common to the all; it must reveal the concretely universal in all the precarious situations which arise for life as both human and non-human.

Since reality is essentially violent, and the atheist cannot shy away from this truth, there is the sense that violation is necessitated by the conditions of the universe. This I think brings us to the heart of radical atheism, allowing us to start to see where the ethical conditions of atheist thought must face. It is, I think, a gentle response to the violent lacerations of reality. Nothingness is impossible tout court. This is because the contingency of things happens. Any event is the negation of nothingness. To think is an exercise in softness and finesse, making apparent the radical contingency and sheer dependency of human mortality.

The demand of vulnerability is placed on the atheist. The atheist is thus like a child walking through a volcano. Whether she responds to the demand of vulnerability is another matter of course, but since violation is imposed on the atheist from her inception by the vibrant conditions of reality, vulnerability becomes the question of being. What opens the human to being is violation. To begin to think the question of being, we must thus think the question of fragility and mortality.

Reality is a teeming torrent of events and happenings, from the atomic vibrations of a sound wave to the gargantuan clamour of icebergs; truth is the approximation of such events within human worlds. Since the atheist is the site of lacerations of reality, the task of a deepened atheistic philosophy is to show and make apparent the operations of truth in the present for the future. The atheist must make the truths of the age appear more decisively and viscerally within the world. This is why truth must always be a commitment for the atheist, since she must always remain sensitive to the order of discovery and invention which allows the human to surpass the mute everyday world that confines it. Reality puts the human in question; being in question opens the universe to the human since the subject is embedded in the multiplicity of things. Furthermore, if the human is in question then prior to anything else, reality imposes a call to impose practice on the reality with which one is faced. Such an existential vulnerability imposes the demand to reflect, select and discriminate out of the bustling presentation of the world of experience, demanding attendance upon the most pressing urgencies and relevant points of our historical positioning.

In this sense the radical atheist is a tragic figure and thus a human figure, one that may only, as Nietzsche proclaimed, affirm the innocence and vulgarity of reality in all its glory. We cannot go as far as Nietzsche ultimately did in accepting his joyful science, since it is only a sad affirmation, one tinged with regret for the impossibility of radical goodness and demarcated by a nascent elitism. The truth of Nietzschean thought is that atheism begins by staring nothingness in the face, and adds the accompanying effort to bring birth and procreation to the absurdity of existence. The Nietzschean human is the negotiator and translator of the irreducibly disparate phenomena making up a life, but the radical atheist must always surpass radical creativity and affirm the common proximity of all things. That the universe is violent is not cause for gloom; it places a demand on the philosopher to explore the possibilities and connections present in this world to all other things that can, are and have happened.

Atheist truth connects our historical world to the murky starlight of reality. Whereas a cynic will luxuriate in the failure of the world, the atheist always holds fast to the precarious contingency that truth exists as the condition of this mess that is existence. Truth again is precisely the axiom that reality is thus. The truth of atheism clings to presenting the logical conditions that make the world around us as it is. This is where Nietzsche was correct: one gets the truths one deserves, and truth is the factual presentation of reality as it is, and can be no other way. To understand, we need to look slightly askew at the world, we need to understand that it is both Dorian Grays, beautiful and ugly. The truth of reality is that it presents itself to us as placid, dumb and inert, but if we focus our senses we can see it persistently disintegrate. This tension between the world around us and the subterranean realm alongside it is that to which the radical atheist strives to bring reflexivity. Reality is Blanchot and Levinas' brutal and anonymous *il y a* which haunts all things; truth slumbers alongside us in all the historical epochs of mortal and material worlds.

What then is the function of the atheist, given that her thought is only the microscopically spewed body odour of a gnat's wing in the midst of the cosmos? The task of the atheist is both to transcend the dialectic of sadness and affirmation, and it is to insert and align possibilities with the tragic structure of existence; it is to explain limits in the face of the infinitely contingent universe around us. The atheist sees that truth is utterly undetermined and unconditioned. It is not a thing or an object that can be picked up or manipulated. Truth must be discerned according to the forces or powers which determine reality as it is and not otherwise.

This is why truth and violence are always intimate lovers. Nietzsche said of philosophy that its task should be to overturn the image of the 'current man', the human only determined by the presence of the now, of the intransigent now. Atheism in the face of currency and brute immediacy must overturn the temptation to become mesmerized by the present, by the crude empirical world before our eyes. Atheism is thus an exercise in cold love, overturning the inevitable lacerations and negations which constitute reality, allowing the blossoming of beginnings of lived life above the ground zero of existence.

Ultimately, the death of atheism is the death of the free human. Positively stated, atheist thought must enamour itself to diminishing any forces of mystification which imprison the human being within the confines of a world, and which only serve to sever the connection between the local and the universal, wherever these powers might reside – be they in a state, an institution, a home, or within the psychological realms of domination and hierarchy that perpetually, and so easily, arise between humans. If the reactive forces of untruth attempt to ground the human in nothing other than its human life, making human life merely present to what it is, then atheism must always play the role of the radical atheist. The radical atheist must entrench in the human heart the human being's place as the midway point between the cosmos and the earth.[24]

The task that the atheist has to answer, for better or worse, therefore pertains to what existing situations allow humans to do, what affirmations can take place, how can we insert possibility into life, what types of practices can be engaged in to bring about new states of affairs, and what level of risk literacy we engage in order to habituate ourselves to the unfolding of reality. The atheism that emerges and departs from Nietzsche is, then, always a form of untimely meditation. The task of the atheist is to depress and disappoint but only in order to unleash the sense that reality itself is defined by possibility, both real and actual. The atheist that does overcome disappointment and sadness can only do so in conjunction with what actually can be achieved, and thus the fragile truth of one's world becomes more palpable. It is incumbent on humans to transcend differences, local myths and fictions, in order to reveal to humans the generic connectivity that lies at the core of existence and hence of all people. The demand on atheism must be to turn localisation and fragmentation into something shameful as much as possible. Indeed, the task of the atheist is to reveal the stupidity that perpetually attempts to re-coordinate thought into the local instead of the all, or the particular into the universal.

Chapter 4

Being Is Time

Time holds little importance for conventional atheism. There are few interventions by atheists or humanists which take up the question of time. This is unusual, since traditionally it is the temporal, the bodily, the mortal and the transient which define the coordinates of this world. It is odd that atheism does not place these concerns at the forefront. There are traditional philosophical reasons for this. The temporal is traditionally associated with flux and change, and therefore with all that is uncertain. Traditionally, if we had to gain a proper grasp of a concept or an object we would have to suspend the question of time. Time involves change, change involves passing, and passing involves uncertainty. If we have uncertainty, we cannot come to have a true knowledge. We cannot ground any object and make it immune to time. Why then should atheism be at all concerned with the question of time? Martin Hägglund, in his coining of radical atheism, states: "If to be alive is to be mortal, it follows that to not be mortal — to be immortal — is to be dead".[25] This statement captures what is most important about time for the radical atheist. It places emphasis on understanding not just the human as a temporal being, but reality itself. The temporal is, therefore, essential for the purposes of understanding a deepened notion of atheism for humans. This is because it negates the possibility of absolute death. What the atheist must understand is that life and death are radically entwined. Understanding atheist human experience requires an understanding of the human as an instance of temporal life. It is through understanding the temporal texture of reality that we can give shape to the human experience of atheism.

Such a determination implies that the fundamental characteristic of being human is that we have a temporal dimension in relation to the organization of the world, a point that tends not to occur in conventional atheist literature. We are temporal beings caught up in the transformative nature of reality and history itself. This is the step Heidegger took. To understand this question, we must first look at Heidegger's later and exceptionally abstruse essay *On Time and Being*. Here Heidegger shifts the inflection of temporality from human temporality to the dispensing or 'giving' of Being itself. This is a fundamental point for existential atheist thought, since it means that Being, reality and the cosmos are a species of temporality themselves. This is absolutely imperative to comprehend since the condition of any existent is temporal through and through. Being is time.[26] This means that any entity that exists is subject to what Hägglund calls the logic of temporal alteration.[27] Here all entities without exception are mortal, and can be understood within the horizon of time; no entity without exception is immune to finitude. But what is it to say that entities are subject to time? This means no being is present in itself and no entities are only themselves.

Whatever being or entity that exists always has an open threefold structure. This threefold structure is the very fabric of Being itself. Time is the three-dimensional elongation of time-past, present and future.[28] In addition, Heidegger adds a fourth dimension of time. This is what he calls 'nearing,' or put another way, the spatialisation of the three times – the unified holding in place, or placing of these times. The fourth dimension of time gathers the other three moments to provide the unified conditions for the taking place of any identity. Despite the abstract formulation, Heidegger's basic effort is to make manifest a structure of occurrence. He is articulating what has to be there for any one thing to happen; what are the conditions, he asks, that must be in place in order for something to occur? In effect, the radical conclusion is that all things are generated from their spatio-temporal coordinates. This is not purely about content or empirical structure, but addresses the transcendental conditions which are necessary to make the dynamics of reality occur: in this instance the spacing or placing of the threefold structure of time. Time-spatialized, or placed, refers to the specific way in which everything is made manifest in relation to other things. Every unique thing is an event, never fully present in itself, but placed according to the general spatio-temporal placing of beings. Only local spatio-temporal occurrences actualize relevant events. Beings cannot be derived from any entity outside of time. The most obvious point that we can take from this for a more profound version of atheism, is that nothing can be derived from something that transcends the coordinates of time and space themselves.

Heidegger, following Husserl's temporal analysis to a degree, thought in many ways that Husserl did not go far enough. Husserl's theory of subjectivity remains too passive, maintaining an artificial separation of internal consciousness and the external world. Heidegger's radical move was to dispense with the question of subjectivity entirely and instead to conceive of the human being as a practical being. If what we are, our being, is temporal, then what are the consequences for our practical activity in the world? The decisive and most generic elements of consciousness reflect the temporal and spatial coordinates of reality itself, since reality and our historical place within it is dynamic and thus has a temporal vector. There is no distinction between what we are and what we do; we are the practices in which we are enmeshed. This is because we *are* time – hence the title of Heidegger's magnum opus *Being and Time*.

Thus Heidegger's philosophy can be re-directed in order to offer a general atheist cosmology. There is no total entity which can transcend the different spatio-temporal events of reality.[29] The divide of inside and outside is no longer applicable. Existence is always outside itself, it is always there, and never needs to scurry elsewhere to find its ultimate cause. More specifically, how does this help us with atheism? In an unusual fashion, I am reading Heidegger backwards here. The structures of events are vital for shedding light on the nature of the human. Traditionally, in Heideggerean scholarship, it is the self-interrogation of the human being that is the privileged site for coming to understand the nature of being. In this instance it is the dispensation of reality that is illuminating. If events are irreducibly temporal, therefore, the human being is generated out of its struggles with the spatio-temporal arrangement of the events and occurrences which make up existence. Heidegger's claim is that philosophy is life, and yet is also utterly concerned with mortality and finitude. There is no separation between thought and the actual enunciation of a human's acts in the world.[30] For Heidegger, this primordial temporality reveals a great deal about human experience. Most significantly, what Heidegger calls *Dasein* cannot provide itself with its own foundation. It encapsulates the human as a fundamentally practical being, one historically determined in time and space. *Dasein* is a philosophical term that avoids the usual baggage of the subject and object. In order to alleviate the separation of the human from the world, Heidegger sees *Dasein* as fundamentally caught up in the world. *Dasein* is thus Heidegger's word for being-in-the-world.

Humans are never given as only themselves; *Dasein* is always ahead of itself or outside of itself. Indeed, the designations 'inside' and 'outside' no longer offer any valid sense of what human life is about. Life is immediately enmeshed in the world. We are simply *there*. Thus the practical orientation of our existence in our everyday struggles is derived from that existence and not from anything else. This is an important point to understand for the atheist in that Heidegger sees questions of temporality as being directly wrapped up in the possibility of lived human existence.

The temporality of existence is, therefore, not the mechanized and quantitative temporality of a succession or a line, but the tangible temporality of life as it happens, where the present arrives from the future and develops from the past. The key to understanding Heidegger's practical ontology is to understand that we are not reducible to what he calls quantitative calendar time – clocks, diaries, minutes, hours, years – but instead that time is ecstatic. We cannot understand the human as derived from subjectivity or derived from objective experiences, nor as being the product of something that remains beyond time i.e. the eternal. The reason for this is that the human relation to time is fundamentally open. The temporal human cannot be reduced or objectified. Humans are essentially open beings because they exist temporally.

Heidegger's major achievement helps the atheist to illuminate the visceral nature of mortal life. The fundamental horizon we face is that the human is constituted first and foremost from its temporality: from finitude and nothing else. Thus any interrogation of any region of reality only can begin when we come to terms with what is most fundamental about our relation to the world – that is, our own being, which is temporal life. While it is not possible to argue that Heidegger could sustain the appellation 'atheist,' philosophical research must remain essentially atheistic for Heidegger.[31] The question all this poses is, what specifically can Heidegger's resources offer the atheist in understanding the nature of reality and the human's place within that reality?

Ecstatic temporality is a process with three dimensions which form an ecstatic unity. His decisive insight is: that what is most generic about being human is the relation with our own temporal existence. Humans have three active dimensions: the past or where we come from, the present or where we are now, and the future, that towards which we are directed. These three spheres are interdependent.[32] They can never be resolved or fully objectified. Humans are always on the way. We are caught up in a present history. In this way, the being of *Dasein* is spatial as much as it is temporal. We are situated within the limits of a world, within a history, and within the organization of things in that world.[33] Our Being-there, Being in the world, means that the human is at an intersection of where we are, what we are, and what we are to become. Humans are always caught in a zone between what we are, where we come from and who we are about to be. Time reveals and always opens and closes off different possibilities. Thus time is inescapable in understanding what it means to be human. *Dasein* is always outside of itself, and is thus generated from its own ecstatic temporality.[34]

Heidegger's insights on the temporal nature of the human being are essential to the atheist. He provides a detailed and practical theory of how humans can have meaning in a meaningless reality. It is precisely because existence is meaningless, i.e. that *Dasein* is contingent, that meaning can take place. In addition, Heidegger's resistance to understanding the human as not reducible to mere properties or things provides us with a wider conception of the human than the scientific conception of man. The human is certainly biologically organized according to physical laws, but alongside this we must also articulate our terrain of enquiry within the existential remit of how a human acts in the world. The decisive point is that the human cannot be determined in itself. Human life is always its activity and in some way more than just its simple physical coordinates. Paradoxically, the atheist must thus understand the human as defined in terms of what it is not. The being of the human is one that cannot transport itself beyond or outside the historical possibilities it has available. In its actions the human always is, and is more than its basic physical reality. *Dasein* is mobilized, always outside itself. Dasein is confronted by numerous possibilities and projects. These cannot be ultimately resolved, each possibility transforms into new ones when some projects become actualized.

What the atheist must take from this analysis is an understanding of the human as a being that exists qua potential, which is to say the potential to be or not to be. Humans exist potentially. Potential is differentiated from actuality. Potential is that which may happen or may come about. The actual is that which is determined. When we actualize ourselves, potentials fade away and become replaced by other potentialities. The human being is that which cannot be reduced to, or determined as, a simple thing, since what exists can only resolve itself into potentiality anyway. This is the point at which the question of a renewed atheism must be staged. The atheist must understand the necessity of time towards making any meaningful claims about the nature of existence. The most radical leap one can take is the leap into what is right before one's eyes. To see the world as it happens is one of the most transfiguring experiences of all. These resources must be drawn on by atheism as they allow us to glimpse the enigmatic and mysterious level of existence, in all its order and contingency, and by extension help us to make sense of how the human is cast into, and exists in its most intimate spaces in the world.

So, what Heidegger offers for a radicalization of atheism is the constitutive and generative nature of mortality. The stakes of atheism must focus on understanding the human as a being that is essentially not determinable in itself. This means that the atheist must confront the existential realities of human being, which is to say, the conditions which make us what we are, the fundamental anxieties which confront us, and the changing nature of our environments. We must radically shift the terrain away from understanding the human in technological terms, as merely mechanistic, as reducible to thinghood or objectification as the vehicle of atheistic thought. While certainly there are many discourses that attempt this, none reach the visceral existential pitch attempted by Heidegger's own idiosyncratic reflections. This is because Heidegger situates the fundamental reality of the human within the mortal and temporal texture of reality in all its vagaries.

Heidegger's great bequest to a possible renewal of atheism is his offer of the conceptual resources for making manifest the developmental and transitive quandaries of a lived human life. Defining the temporal texture of human life bestows upon atheist reflection the generic conditions of existence, those things which organize all other events. This is certainly something that naturalistic and humanistic accounts of atheist life lack. If we look to Heidegger we can begin to complement the naturalistic accounts with an existential account. A meaningful existential analysis is basically organized around certain key fundamental junctures of human existence. Heidegger does not speak about individuals but about the generic features of every individual's existence. These features can help us to refocus the commitments of atheism. But what are these moments that are essential?

Firstly, what is decisive is that we can take from Heidegger the way he transforms the notion of transcendence. The idea that the self can step outside itself is a generic concern of human thought, and it is important that the atheist finds ways of speaking to it. What is most decisive is that there is no singular, exceptional or momentary transcendence. Instead, transcendence is always the case, and thus paradoxically is no longer an issue. This can be described as a horizontal transcendence rather than a vertical transcendence. It is towards what is immediate, towards the world, our projects, towards our environs, towards others. Transcendence is in some way a philosophical embarrassment for Heidegger. Transcendence is no longer needed as we usually understand it; if we are always in the thick of things, we just need to shift our vision slightly in order to reveal to ourselves the manifold ways in which reality comes alive. It is transcendence in immanence that distinguishes Heidegger's ecstatic thought, and thus the traditional split between transcendence and immanence is set aside. We are just beings in the world in all its vicissitudes and vagaries, struggling to overcome our temporal and spatial positioning.

Heidegger fortifies this logic by concentrating on the theme of death, which, in its own way, illuminates and brings relief into the nature of existence. Philosophical thought must begin and end with life in the mortal and the mortal in life. Humans are beings that are temporal. Therefore, we are beings that pass, and thus we pass in and out of existence. Humans are finite and limited by death. Death is the moment when all possibilities reach their end. Our existence as taking up different possibilities is characterized by the selection and forsaking of various possibilities where and when we exist. We live in a world filled with possibilities to a greater or lesser extent. Death casts the most meaning on these possibilities once it seeps into our existence. Death, Heidegger claims, is the impossibility of all possibility for *Dasein*.

The truth of our existence, from birth to death, only ever comes to fruition when death finalizes all the possibilities, choices, actions and projects that we have undertaken. This is a valuable insight moreover, as it contributes to alleviating the empirical/humanistic divide that sadly fractures twentieth-century philosophy. The truth of life is its temporal and mortal nature from birth to death, and this truth provides the conditions upon which the human can gain the broadest and most truthful sense of how reality hangs together. It is within this background that we can engage with others, see what is really and truthfully important and place ourselves within the irrefutable facts of existence. Heidegger remains thoroughly philosophical in this way. Atheism must support his insight that the meaningful occurs when the facts of life are in conjunction with what actually is. The lived factual nature of the world must remain ever-decisive for atheism.

Inasmuch as death defines and haunts the phenomenon of life, allowing the truth of the world to surge forth to meet us, it is the world itself which presents the human with the most palpably immediate existential moment. Heidegger presents the world we inhabit as being full of luminosity and darkness. Heidegger writes within the tradition of the Greek tragedians. Our world is underworld and this-world at once, a transfiguring assemblage of the radically mysterious and the weirdly banal. What a renewal of atheism requires is the recognition that the human is defined immediately by the world it inhabits. This is more than saying we are moulded by our upbringing; we need to say more than that the world is just there. This is the crassest form of behaviourism and remains an obvious case of taking the empirical world for granted. Such is the tyranny and limitation of common sense. The world before our eyes is much more interesting and transformative than that. We are beings-with-world, we engage with the world and we transform it as much as it transforms us. We are defined by our immediacy and distance from the world. It is certainly true to say that atheists are traditionally concerned with the world and with being involved in it. But it is rare that it can be framed in the rich way that Heideggerean resources offer, giving due attention to the limits of our interaction with our history, our desires to overcome the confines of our existence, and the extent to which we sometimes overreach ourselves and attempt to stave off mortal life by gambling on the eternal.

Another key moment that Heidegger offers the atheist is the meaning and joy humans can take from trying to accord themselves with the transformative nature of existence. We cannot forsake the brutal fact that we are always outside of ourselves. We are here, there, concerned with the past and future and how they impact on the present. Mortal life entails that atheism must luxuriate in the events of existence; we are most attuned to ourselves when we are at ease with movement and the occurrences which befall us. As Heidegger argues, "Along with the sober anxiety which brings us face to face with our individualized ability-to-be, there goes an unshakable joy."[35] There is a poignant moment of atheist illumination in evidence here. While we can never excise anxiety and the nothingness at the core of existence, we can take sheer delight in the way the world is, how it is comes to be and in relation to things that we can bring into being. The radical atheist sees the mortal as a being of both light and shade, and filled with the need to love the mere fact that things occur as they do, and as they merely are. If the atheist listens to Heidegger, the human is always already committed to a generic form of love. This is more than basic love of another person; it is love for the fragile and precarious order of the world as it comes to be, come what may.

Why is love a trajectory we can take from Heidegger for the atheist? Firstly, it is necessary, as there is very little atheist foregrounding of the questions of love and mortal life. Secondly, it is because it is decisive for understanding the existential human being. Love is the intersection between time, location, truth and existence. Love is the movement that allows connection to the truth of what is happening: to ourselves, our world, their world and the world itself. Heidegger can thus offer to atheist discourse the transparent manifestation of the truth of the world. To bear fidelity to this truth is to come to understand how our events, projects, politics, civil society *et al.* sometimes gently and sometimes violently penetrate our own life. Love transforms our specific position in the world into a fidelity to all that is happening. In a sense, to be an atheist is to have a divided yet sober love for all the possibilities that the world lays at our feet.

The truth of mortal life is that it is essentially divided, and outside itself. But this is precisely the condition that allows the human being to invest and engage in any project to transform the co-ordinates of its life and world. While perhaps Heidegger overestimates the ability of the human to gather itself, he does make apparent that the task of existence is to remain committed to the events which love illuminates in our lives. This is exceptionally important for the atheist since it demonstrates how the metaphysical and objective elements of the human thinking coincide. Truth is a comrade of love, and always remains more than mere neutral facts, or objectivity. Truth, or what Heidegger would call *alēthia*, implies that the human is contingent, and therefore open to the needs of others as much as the world come what may, whether in times of weariness or alacrity.

Truth for the atheist should thus be configured as entwined with the logical and metaphysical illumination of reality and our participation in it. The logical condition of truth in this regard is temporal: everything that comes to be, by virtue of being there, is true. The facts of that matter about how the world is arranged can be discerned after the fact. Reality, and our stake and concern for it, share a common fate; the truth of being or reality realizes us as being there, in the thick of things. Thus atheism must attempt to join the metaphysical with the natural and the bodily with the inert. In addition to this meeting of the metaphysical and the natural, we can begin to see what makes the conditions of ethical and political life possible. There is in the human a desire and movement for truth, but a truth tempered by the vicissitudes of life and a truth which can bring things into existence. The human is a being that transforms. It coordinates its limited resources and takes joy in the creation of reality. There is a desire for an ease of movement. Thus the atheist must find her imperative in struggling with the truth of reality. Atheism in its revitalized form must present a mode of reflection that allows itself to be perturbed and turbulent, but by the same stroke it must delight in reflecting on how the world is organized, how it can be re-organized with regard to the things of the world and the beings of the world. If atheism is to emerge into a radical atheism, we must define its thought as the delight in the desire to have proportionate aims and relative projects. It must be defined by the production of human affairs, of human discourse in the visceral relation of innumerable things and events.

Human discourse is never absolute in itself; it is defined by the sheer relationality of innumerable events. The atheist's desires to change things must form with respect to the factual *and* lived truth of the world. Facts limit our ethical conjectures of what is possible, but they are also by necessity the beginning of how we can transform our shared experience. In this sense, what is truthful always has a temporal vector for human production and creation; that which Heidegger calls facticity, the factual lived truth of the world, is, therefore, always the condition and limitation from which a radical atheism can begin in the binding of truth and existence. Things are, and truthfully are thus, and that is the ground where we can begin to make things otherwise. Time and truth wait for no human, and are thus the most basic and generic resources we must take up in order to negate the nothingness and destruction that is always a possibility for our world. Heidegger's idea that the human is naturally outside itself implies that possibility is always enmeshed in our experience of lived factuality.

Once the atheist can begin to grasp these points she will be able to address questions of meaning, values and solidarity in a more universal fashion. Thus the 'possible' is a discourse that atheism should take up even further. Given the sheer contingency of where we find ourselves in the world, whether we are a bored desk jockey or languishing in prison, the importance of possibility is paramount to what we are. In this sense, the atheist is a being that projects beyond itself into its temporal future. The human is always oriented towards the things that it is not. Paradoxically, for atheism, what Heidegger brings to thought is the idea that transcendence is immanence. We no longer have to teeter on the edge of Sören Kierkegaard's abyss; the most powerful and transforming leap of all is into the everyday world, the sheer fact that things are happening around us, and into commitment to the projects we share with the others who populate that world.

Most importantly, what these reflections offer the radical

atheist is an understanding of the human being as a being that is within its utmost experience of possibility: a being that cannot but negate nothingness. The human holds the chance to refute nihilism with each of its actions. It has the ability to resist objectification, i.e. the act of turning humans into things. The human stripped of temporal possibility is the thing, that is to say the inhuman, it is that which is dead. While there are many debates within Heidegger scholarship about the adequacy of Heidegger's response to nihilism, the central point that atheism should take from him is his continual reflection on the importance of possibility. This amounts to placing at the core of philosophical reflection what humans can do to achieve the maximal liberation from the irretrievably negative aspects of human existence. The best name for all the temporal modes of human existence, our transcendence, our anxiety and luxuriating in the face of our lived possibilities, is freedom. The human in its truest expression is the freedom from, and challenge to, the caprice of destruction and negation. The human being negates the present and rises above the reduction of humans to things. Time reveals the finitude of beings and reality itself. *Dasein* in its temporal being is the being that is open toward its possibilities and is thus a being that is at once both freedom and constraint.

In summation, the value of Heidegger's account of temporality, of the human being as the past, present and future, as a being that does not offer itself the shelter of a ground, offers the atheist the possibility of thinking about the richness of existential truth. That we are mortal, and we participate in reality along with the finitude of other beings, shows us that our manner of meaningfully understanding reality is a case of understanding the movement of reality itself. This discourse is exceptionally attractive for a transformed atheism, as it offers the atheist an outlet for talking about meaning and purpose whilst facing the truth of death, mortality and the chaos of the universe without taking itself too seriously. Mortal life and the possibilities that it announces entail that 'meaning' is inserted as a possibility from the beginning, even if it is forever split and redirected in itself. The lesson which Heidegger teaches us is that it is precisely because of the utter contingency of being that 'meaning' is there all the time. That there is 'purpose', 'the meaning of life', 'direction,' a 'plan for,' can only come into being when the relentless reality of temporal alteration reveals the world and others and our projects alongside themselves in the lived factuality of existence. Hence what we are and what we turn into are entwined or, as David Webster puts it, how we are and what we are to become are both sides of the same coin.[36] The truth of existence is the emerging of our time in a world that erases our impositions of permanence upon it. The task of the human within this realm of finitude is to attune itself freely to the being of the world, to the truth of what is happening in the most appropriate ways possible in a collective effort towards understanding the most contested values, their origin and what actually matters in our ethical and political situations.

Chapter 5

The Common

Heidegger shows the atheist the importance of expressing the generic conditions of human existence. Thus, the next step for recalibrating atheism is to try and think a bit more about what such a common life might look like and what values atheism must necessarily espouse. The true values of atheism are so blindingly obvious that they need bluntly restating. Atheism, if it is to be at all meaningful, requires such things as the cultivation of a collective life; it requires commitment to overcoming torture, slavery, murder, rape, inhumane treatment of others, needless domination, indulgence in vain hierarchy, and performing ethnic cleansing and genocide. The more interesting philosophical point is the reason why these values exist. The answer depends on what I claim is the 'common,' which is to say common life or the public sphere of existence, discourse upon which is totally lacking in contemporary versions of atheism. By the common, I mean the generic conditions of human existence, without which we would not be able to participate: the many things that all humans meet in their life in this world. The aforementioned values can only come into existence when a common and generic dimension of human existence is present. It is only when we see that the cruelties listed above are not just assaults on individuals – as horrific as this is – but on our humanity, that we can begin to think the most real and authentic ethical and political consequences of atheism.

It is the task here to enrich this notion of the common for atheism. It is because common humanity is not articulated enough in standard accounts of atheism, such as those by Dawkins, Harris, Dennett and Hitchens, that we are obliged to turn to other resources.[37] If atheism is to mean anything, it must articulate the common and generic conditions of humankind, the moment when we can see what our individual existence is enmeshed in and what has a stake in humanity as a whole. Atheists need a much more dynamic and broader understanding of the universal dimensions of human experience. In this chapter I will begin to sketch out some of the key philosophical moments necessary to understanding common existence.

Paolo Virno has provided some valuable insights into how we might conceptualize our common being.[38] Virno is important for a radicalized interpretation of atheism because of his acknowledgement of the contingency of human states of affairs and the perpetual universalist dispositions that are always at stake, irrespective of any postmodern celebration of difference. He lists three moments at which our generic pre-individual being might be considered.[39] These are important moments for the renewal of atheism since they offer us a way through which the human can depersonalize itself. This starkly deviates from traditional atheism which can ultimately be defined as a moment of belief in the status of evidential claims. How does Virno's de-individuation proceed? Firstly, there is the pre-individual biological basis of the species. These are dispositions generated by our sensory, motor, perceptual and neurological life. There is a sense of the transcendental to this claim. It is never the content that we experience when we see or hear or touch; it is instead that we have a body. Virno describes this as an anonymous representation that requires a shift in awareness in order to be understood. When we feel, we feel and sense along the lines of the anonymous pronoun *one sees, one touches, one hears*.[40] Secondly, language for Virno is pre-individual. Language too is anonymous; it is cheap and ubiquitous, as well as vital and therefore invaluable. In this, Virno is of a mind with Jacques Derrida's *pharmakon*. Language belongs to everybody and nobody at one and the same time. Thirdly, there is the historical condition of humanity. *One* is positioned within certain modes of production and arrangement. The labour process ensures that one possesses *one's* "...universal requisites of the species: perception, language, memory, and feelings."[41] The human being is an 'open manifestation': it is specific and generic simultaneously, and it is radically historical and thrown into the sensuous conditions it shares with all other humans, but is never absolutely defined by them.

The most decisive way of articulating the common is that it is abstract. The common cannot be conceived simply in terms of the empirical or subjective content of human experiences. It is not just that we experience *this* or *that* thing, but that there remains a generic dimension to human experience. All humans experience common needs and dependencies in different ways. Certainly all individual humans have subjective experiences; however, this could not take place without certain conditions being in place. The trouble with current atheist discourse is that the articulation of such a dimension is lamentably lacking. Contemporary atheists consider the locus of human dignity as primarily resting on the liberty of the individual. It is very important to note that this does not mean that existing atheism is not interested in the collective dimensions of human experience, but rather that any such form of co-operation must be premised on rationalism, progress, individual responsibility; the meaning of atheism is always in some way 'my meaning'.

It is crucial for atheism, then, to complement Enlightenment values with the common. Virno, in his own way, begins to see how this is possible by reclaiming what Karl Marx calls 'species-being'.[42] Marx's atheism relies on understanding how the human is in some way a contingent being-in-the-world, reliant on both its animal nature and the simultaneous attempt to overcome that nature. Indeed this is why his work can never fall within the category of scientific determinism; human nature can never be fully understood as merely an aggregate of its properties, but is instead the product of its 'species-being,' which is to say how it is embedded in material social relations and sensuous embodied life.[43] Species-being, then, is the activity of common human life along with, and over and above, both our animal and cultural life. The common is the universal vector of individual human lives; it is the irreducible yet active question inserted into all human activity, announced when human beings transform their inescapable animal life into collective life. Thus the human being's being-in-the-world is a being of desires, basic needs and struggles: food, shelter, health, water, sexuality, and the all-round development of possibility.

The common is the generic and inescapable human disposition to cultivate its specific and basic needs with regard to the common life of the human species.[44] The reason Marx's analysis of species-being is so important for any atheism worthy of the name is that it realizes the sheer contingency of the human in the universe, along with the concurrent desire to impose on that universe something durable and lasting. Marx is so important because his work offers the atheist a way of understanding the atheistic position as both an individual and as an inter-dependent being. The lesson the atheist can learn from Marx is to remain mindful of the vagaries of existence, while seeing that the human is a being-in-the-world, a historical being that is the product of its times, and which involves relative transformation and change. Such transformation, however, does not imply a relativisation of human beings; the historical production of human beings implies generic struggles common and meaningful to all. The struggle to eke out an amenable existence from the contingency of life is universal to all and ineliminable. Any atheism, if it is to be meaningful universally, must by definition give an adequate account of this, contesting and demonstrating how humans transform the contingency of their material surroundings whilst determining their own nature, thereby uniting the scientific vision of the world with the lived one.

In true Marxist fashion, authentic atheism cannot be reducible or made co-extensive to contemporary forms of capitalism, since capitalism is essentially a particular ideological movement. Capitalism eternalizes the human being in an atemporal 'now', having no sense of lived events and no empathic illumination of the factual location of humans in the world. Capitalism in its essence is devoted to emptying the common of any meaning in order to achieve the chimera of a bland homogeneity. More specifically, atheism cannot be capitalist because authentic atheism is committed to understanding the real material needs and necessities of vulnerable humans. The main atheist argument against liberal and capitalist societies is, therefore, that in such societies there is an equivalence drawn between the human and money. The abstract point is that humans can thus be thought of as units or things. Why would this be the case? It is because humans can be monetized and valuable insofar as they behave like money, where all units are the same. This stands as the greatest systematic perversion of the common.

What type of human being must the atheist being then be? The atheist human is a finite and mortal being, one that strives to impose necessity on the accidental manifestation of the human being on earth. The human is both dependent on its animal nature and receptive to the transformation of that very nature. The atheist human is thus a habitual and contingent being as it faces the world and takes up projects to transform its existence. It has a suffering, limited and creaturely existence which at once names the tendencies and abilities to verify its essential power in order to overcome this existence. Without thinking of the human in this way our current form of atheism is irretrievably nothing. The human undoubtedly has an animal side, bequeathed with animal needs, natural tendencies and dispositions and deeply embodied with responsive reactions to its surroundings. What atheism must delineate is precisely how human animality is animal but at once culturally and civilly transformed in an effort to envisage specific life.[45]

Another decisive point in articulating the common is that we should not see it as a 'thing'. The generic conditions of human experience are simply mechanical or can be understood as a unique object. The human as an open manifestation is not an essence that resists the activities of human struggle. The human being is a series of projects and struggles in perpetual attempts to transform its environment in the effort to provide shelter and to fulfil basic needs. As with Heidegger, what is important is that despite different types of human experience we can think the generic determination of human existence. We can show what is common irrespective of one's situation within the world. In opposition, we can say that the common is the direct expression of what Jacques Rancière calls equality. For Rancière, lived political life is always at hand, ready to be engaged with. While certainly there are hierarchies and different group identities which exist, this never precludes the possibility of a radical 'we' arising. Authentic political engagement cannot be attributed to any single section of the population. The lesson the atheist can learn from this is that the political distribution of people must adhere to what Rancière calls counting the countless.[46] Democratic politics is that which counts: it counts who belongs here, who belongs there, it categorizes according to income and class, according to the possession of objects and means. Politics in this light is based on mere quantification and instrumentalisation. This is absolutely a crucial moment for atheism, beyond which atheism must move.

If politics is based on quantification and instrumentalisation, this gives politics a 'scientific' aura, seemingly based on some empirical justification. Thus, if politics is to be relevant to all, then in some meaningful way it must commit to discerning what is achievable. For the atheist, atheism cannot bring to fruition any of its aims or goals if it does not take on nihilism, and thus the creeping habituations which humans acquire where the debilitating thought is entrenched, where nothing is achievable or possible. While contemporary atheism should be commended for criticizing the pernicious aspects of totalitarianism, it cannot complete its mission until it resists a culture of nothingness and destruction to replace it. A deepened atheism is best-placed to do this, as we have argued all along, in its drive to negate nothingness. Atheism must resist the urge to commit itself to the now, to the currency of the human, to a detemporalized existence. The historical positioning of the human being is always ecstatically geared beyond itself. The task of politics is to realize how this manifests itself optimally as a common yet precarious aspiration.

Thus, for the atheist, a renewed engagement with the common is decisive, because the common announces all that is fresh and vital in politics. In essence, atheism must commit to a democratization of democracy. Democratic politics, as things stands, is essentially hollowed out – it is devoted to questions of number and quantitative policy. What politics commits people to never amounts to more than a question of statistics, surveys, happiness indices, representative focus groups, the mass technologisation of desires and the universalization of corporate discourse. While certainly there are hierarchies and different group identities which exist, this never precludes the possibility of a radical 'we' coming into being. The common denotes the contingency of all identities and the manner in which they can be exposed to each other. Following Rancière, we can take the common to be errant and spectral. It is contingent, holding only a limited durable position within any social edifice. The task of authentic politics is to engage with giving voice to those who need to be heard on an equal footing. This is not the only natural limit; the human comprises many other limits of which atheism must acknowledge the truth. The permeable limit of body and world, the limitation of ambition, the contingency of wealth, the limits of mastery, and the limitations that beset narcissism and egoism; the human is perpetually placed in precarious and vulnerable positions, drawing sustenance from that which is beyond itself. The atheist must remain committed to finding a way of articulating a vision of the good life, one in tension with the common conditions and limitations experienced by all humans in the context of the broader world, in order to articulate the possibility of liberation from any form of domination structured by inequality and exploitation.

The task for the atheist is to offer a meaningful and visceral account of 'the good life.' The most important task for the atheist of the twenty-first century will be to define the common more expansively. We must transcend the fragmented, particular and sectional interests of what comprises the good life, and express the generic conditions of human life which transcend competing schemes of value. More importantly in this context, atheism must overcome its traditionally apolitical stance. While atheism certainly makes political interventions, it does not in a sustained fashion define the most urgent and necessary forms of organizing the world and the political organization of society in general. What a more radical and existential account of atheism can offer is where the question of humanity, and humanity in question, is most at stake in relation to the historical transformations of biology, labour, and language.

Once the common destiny of humanity is at stake, we can no longer only reduce the question of politics to economics. Thus the atheist must perpetually confront the reduction of human experience to gross homogeneity. This is most evident, as we saw with Nietzsche, in the equivalency of the human with currency, where the individual is atomized, reduced to mere units. In this way, the truest form of atheism is anathema to the most benighted exploitations of neoliberal capitalism. Why is radical or existential atheism not reducible to capitalism? This is because atheism, in its articulation of the common, is committed to understanding the sheer contingency and temporality of the human being. The human being is a contingent being. Certainly money is contingent, as Marx suggested when he said it makes all that is solid melt into air. However, the human is contingent in a different way. Capital is ruthless in its drive to homogeneity. The human finds the common in the different activities of which its life consists. This is supported by the basic fact that economic prosperity does not necessarily lead to a happy or good life. Human contingency is really more than basic transience. It is constructing that which is durable and robust in the face of, and in spite of, the contingency of the cosmos.

Atheism must recuperate itself and combat all forms of political fragmentation. The resources which the philosophical tradition of existential atheism offers are a vision of common life in terms of the mutual recognition of need and struggle. Such a transformed atheism will offer a stark and challenging view of human existence, one where the human is always without ultimate recourse, but is able truthfully to discern the precariousness and fragility of collective human existence, and the points at which that vulnerability is exploited by the cult of hierarchy. For the atheist, the common must hold an address to the all that transcends sectional interests and differences. Here it is imperative to distinguish the difference between atheism and liberal individualism. Atheism, once radicalized, cannot account for the common in terms of competing sets of values, individual preferences, and the offer of the political contestation of one ideology over another. All these are ultimately negations of the political. Instead atheism must, as I have argued throughout this book, and as Nietzsche instantiated in *The Gay Science*, attempt to overcome nihilism, or to negate the culture of negation and the production of nothingness. A radicalized atheism posits the lived factual life of the political in opposition to modern, economically-driven societies. For the atheist, the articulation of the common must configure the collective existence of human beings as free in conjunction with fellow humans. The existential atheist is understanding of the political and directly perceives that the common is always a question for whatever political intervention is at stake.

To say that the common may be perverted is to acknowledge the very fact that it is not immune to alteration or contingency. Indeed this makes the common all the more precious and worthy of struggle. The common, it must be repeated, is not something inactive and inert. It is, as Marx suggested, the universal urge to turn our contingent world into something meaningful and sensuously agreeable. Hence from the perspective of the activity of the human, the common is the ineliminable struggle with collective human mortality and finitude in the material world, an urge that can only be met within the collective dimensions of human experience. Both the affirmation and confirmation of common life comprises the sensible verification of our precarious but universal experience. The common is not a thing: it resists reification, it is not a given. It is always there insofar as it can be practised and established truthfully at all times. What is important is how it reveals that the true mission of any atheism is to overcome nihilism, or the ever-increasing production of nothing.

That the common may be taken up again and again in new forms within any historical configuration in existence illustrates the ability of the human to resist the currency of the human, or the human's commitment to an atemporal present. The common is thus not measurable, nor is it some far-removed ideal or goal that can be infinitely deferred: it is there ready to be taken up. The radical atheist must see that atheism is only truly atheism when it is relevant to all people and their material struggles with the world. The common urge of humans is to see that their being-in-the-world is not a mere problem to be solved or a policy to be administered, but instead that the question of their essential dignity and common aspiration may be maintained in all cases. The common is not something that is dispensed from on high, or earned through individual constructions of meaning: it exists already, to be affirmed and worked through. The contingency of the universe is reflected in the contingency of the human in the world. To consolidate the actuality of human existence, any atheist political intervention must presuppose the radical commonality of all humans.

Certainly different humans have different needs, but if atheism is to be taken seriously then it must challenge the false perpetuity of social orders, assert their contingency, and radically affirm the sensuous and yet alien commonality of all humans with all other humans. By acknowledging the importance of the contingency of human life, and the essential weakness of identities, the atheist can acknowledge the universality of mortal life and human suffering. Human beings suffer, then they turn suffering into a virtue, and such a state of affairs must be avoided at all costs. The precarious overcoming of suffering is something that we must begin to see through the potential for creating equality within any identity. A transformed atheism must adopt the language of radical solidarity or remain meaningless to humans. In this way we can acknowledge the radical historicity of human reality.

As with Nietzsche, and for an articulation of the common, it is the greatest task of the atheist to disavow the nihilistic and relativistic drive for 'personalization.' This means that one must transgress the morass of the postmodern celebration of differences and their interminable negotiations by establishing how regulative normative equivalencies must be drawn. It is decisive that atheism begins not in personal rejection, but within the framework of equivalences which institutes the relations of commonality that are present to the world: sensuous life, facts, struggle, linguistic representations, possibility and violence, to name but a few. However, we must understand that irrespective of the lived moment when we are engaged in these things we are still always defined by the precarious illumination and open manifestation of our singular-universal experience. Sartre articulates this most eloquently and acutely in *Existentialism and Humanism*. In that famous text, he describes the generic determination of being human:

> But what never vary are the necessities of being the word, of having to labour and to die there. These limitations are neither subjective nor objective, or rather there is both a subjective and objective aspect of them. Objective, because we meet with them everywhere and they are everywhere recognisable; and subjective because they are lived and are nothing if man does not live them...[47]

What is common to the human being is the absolute nature of our historical limitations. All human beings who realize themselves through their actions are also recognizing in themselves a commitment to humanity. To be free is to be common. To assert one's freedom is to recognize the liberty of others. Sartre's radical and much-neglected point is that there is no difference between human liberation in our historical positions and in our universal species-being.[48] Sartre's singular universal is the kernel of understanding generic atheism. Far from the usual half-baked descriptions of Sartre as espousing a personalist voluntarism, his atheism must be taken to be motivated by a singular-universal experience. When we engage individually in projects we do not choose ourselves – when we choose authentically – we cannot but depersonalize ourselves. My choices cannot live up to themselves; this is the burden of responsibility. Freedom becomes truly mitigated, and thus becomes freer than ever. When I choose myself I choose as a humble representative of all humanity. A generic anonymity haunts my individuality.

The reflections I receive from the world accuse me and beckon me to make the world a better place. My responsibility extends me beyond the cult of the individual. Everything I do is fashioned in an image of humanity. Whatever I do, wherever I am acting, when I go to college, get on a bus, pick up the milk, attend a funeral, get married, I am self-presenting a version of how humanity should be. One's existence stands accused, and cannot be lived up to, yet always at the same stroke we must strive to do just this. The unmistakable universal dimension of human existence haunts us from our inception. One's very existence is a case for what humans can, should and might be. For Sartre, "Everything happens to all humans as if the entire human race had their eyes fixed upon it and regulated its conduct accordingly."[49] This incredible but precarious freedom defines how we are fundamentally free only when we choose for ourselves a picture of what humanity should be like. Sartre has no doubt a stark vision of the human: we are left alone without excuses. When fashioning myself I fashion humanity, I fashion the state of humanity. Atheism must build itself upon the rock of what all humans do with their freedom.

Sartre, at least on this point, neatly ties together the themes of this book. Atheism must begin with the contingency of a vulnerable and chaotic world. It must discern the actions of the human being in its ongoing efforts to make permanent and durable structures; it must fight against the foreclosure of human possibility. The zenith of our sensuous and collective possibility is free depersonalization with regard to its stake in the common destiny of humanity. One cannot be free until one sees that the freedom of others is always at hand. The generic stakes of human existence are always present; this is a spatial and temporal, localized and historical composition which cannot but have sentient and universal dispositions always ready to be taken up.[50] For atheism, the human as the self-enclosed arbiter of an ethical community needs to be contested in favour of depersonalization and universalization. This is not to say that the way we come to the generic does not begin with reflective thought and awareness – only that what we are, and where we are going, may be more meaningfully considered in connection to the facts of the world and how they situate us actively in the world.

The common is not for any particular sectional interest or group; it represents the whole rather than different and fractured identities. Hence the atheist, in an effort to engage in solidarity and a depersonalized universalism, must always begin from the accepted fate of human contingency. To instantiate the collective stakes of human beings is always a process of dis-identification and hence an exposure to different groups, different narratives of emancipation and liberations, and the places, times, and spaces they occupy. Atheism as the discourse on the generic contingency of human life and all it elicits for self-awareness becomes first philosophy. The common cannot be objectified, it cannot be reduced and it has no content. It can only be taken up again and again. It is for this reason that philosophy more than contains the ghost of atheism to reach its fullest historical and ethical expression.

That collective humanity is at stake must be the most defining moment of existential atheism. This is indeed Sartre's clear point. For him, we do not have an essence when our humanity becomes important. As I have argued throughout this book, the human being is a contested being, it is a being filled with its own non-being and the limitations imposed upon it by the world and others. Thus, what is common to all humans is the perpetual contestation of their own nature. This generic limitation shows to the atheist that all instances of human existence begin from the limitations imposed by the world and other human beings. This is not a negative description of humans' relations with each other, or a Hobbesian war of all against all. Humanity only takes its impetus from the common necessity of bringing forth its essence and what is most important and meaningful for it, in direct relation to its struggle for a just organization of the world. Existential atheism places the human in a stark and contingent cosmos, imposing on all the universal desire to offer the most just organization of human society.

For the atheist then, the question of the 'common' is unsurpassable and unavoidable in developing its resources for dealing with the real material problems the world faces: overpopulation, environmental catastrophe, war and economic exploitation. That the common is unsurpassable for the atheist resides in the fact that the problems humanity faces are existential problems that affect us as a species. We can no longer crudely characterise existentialism as juvenile individualism, especially in the face of the searing fact that the essence of humanity has never been more contested. It is contested universally, irrespective of space, time and identity. Thus the atheist's response to this contestation is the most vital intellectual need of our age. Thus far atheism has not been sufficient. To be sufficient – to be reclaimed – atheism has to articulate that which is most common, the generic material needs that are relevant to all.

Conclusion

Such themes as mortal life, transformation, the centrality of time, violence and the universal struggles of human experience underline a trajectory which can be described as metaphysical atheism. The resources of such philosophers as Virno, Heidegger, and Sartre can present an ontological challenge to the atheist to make our language meaningful, relevant, and entwined with the transformative practices of everyday life. In opposition to this is the totalitarian metaphysics of the eternal. Albert Camus provides perhaps the best example of this. In *The Rebel*, he presents a critique of rebellion for rebellion's sake. Camus opposed all types of eternalisation, and this is why he remains important: he can provide atheistic philosophy with a restless curative to the temptation to absolutise its human and historical origin, in the face of an absurd existence where totality is impossible from its inception.[51] Camus critiques the ethical posturing of liberal academics, fascist demagoguery, rational idolatry and the utopian messianism of Stalinism. He provides one of the most chilling examples of the dangerous consequences of such posturing, in what may be called the logic of the guillotine. Camus draws an analogy between the nemesis of the French monarch, with its very precision and incisive logic, and the glorification of science and reason themselves. The guillotine marked the first instantiation of systematic and mechanized death. The revolutionaries were able to cut and mutilate at will without any opposition, guilt or contestation; bodies became interchangeable units with no distinction or importance. The rationalist revolutionaries became idols to their own transgression, the epitome of the desire to instantiate eternal purity on earth. In essence, the mingling of death and mechanics marks the worst tendencies of reason. Camus's metaphysical atheism thus points to the type of thought that a radical atheist must overcome in any context. This is the seduction of the hubristic, the wantonly cruel and callous, and most of all, the attempt to circumscribe the historical possibilities and limitations of human beings. The logic of the guillotine is thus always exclusional and hierarchical. It deifies or eternalizes a particular human community over others.

The drive to totality and meaningless systematization resists the essential temporal nature of human experience, the common struggles and failures of life and the diminishing of the possibilities of human self-determination. The hubristic desire for eternity immobilizes the future and past dimensions into a system of pre-arranged and irrelevant facts, thereby denying the human agent its historical possibilities. If humans are temporal beings then they cannot be absolute, which implies that we are beings who are precarious, contingent, bodily, forgetful, prone to madness and irrationality, as well as desirous and just downright messy beings who are half in love with truth. There is an important ethical point at stake here. Once we realize that human freedom is at one with temporal and mortal life, the implication is that we have a contingent and mortal body, a body which lives and attempts to stave off death with survival. None of what we engage in is permanent or eternal, not satisfactions, not achievements, not our vanity, our expectations or material acquisitions. In fact, the only way any of these can acquire meaning is if they are marked by death. Things are all the more valuable because they pass; they are more precarious, precious and vulnerable. That we experience mortal life precisely places us within the horizon of that which is most authentically precious: the fact that humans are developmental, open and receptive to the question of the collective fate of humanity. It is because of this contingency that we are ethical, not in spite of it. If this were not the case then the human being would not meet any challenge, risk or contestation; it would be bereft of exposure to the possibilities or the ability to self-develop.[52] To live mortally is to live along with death, it is to live along with a sense of one's own species-being and inherent vulnerability, as well as to remain mindful of the realistic possibilities available to change our situations. Our happiness is not permanent. It is visceral, material and experiential, only possible because of exposure from its outset. Without loss, or some kind of suffering, we would quite literally become fixated, like things needing to be 'fixed,' in a plethora of frozen and static obsessions. To engage with the rough mess of life is to engage in just that: living well along with sex, food, art, music, values and the ever-precarious sense of the universal life of being human. Likewise in political terms, the most just human community is the one which remains attuned to the precarious and historical becoming of its citizens, one which strives to make and realize that community, and to ensure the ubiquitous conditions of human flourishing.

To embrace existential thought is to oppose the desire for states of satisfaction and infinite repose where humans are exempt from wanting anything. Pursuing infinite repose brings things to a stop; humans annul care in an effort to stave off our most palpable finitude, placing us in the grasp of the desire for power in order to fill whatever void we find at our core. The vainest grip of human torments arises from this fear: the tyrant, petty or significant, who tries to totalize their power or the stalker who remains obsessed and fixated on one person. Any atheism worthy of its name must attempt to overcome this purgatorial cycle of purity and violent acquisition, in order to acknowledge the necessary violence and drama of human life. All of this is not to demand throwing the baby out with the bathwater when it comes to scientific enquiry. It is only to point out that scientific atheism, if it is to come to full fruition, must engage with the reality of human existence and its political struggle for the organization of a collective and flourishing human society.

Radical atheism must be an exercise in open manifestation. This is a phenomenological point. The task of a radicalized form of atheism must always be an exercise in making visible. This is the most simple and complex task for the philosopher. The atheist must engage with the beauty and austerity of the world of science, while simultaneously taking a radical leap of faith into the world around her. There is nothing more shocking than stepping out of the confines of the banal and habitual flow of our daily lives into the philosophical vision of the everyday as it shimmers before us. The atheist must view the world slightly askew, maintaining at once the brutal scientific view of reality and the precarious illumination of existence. This is why the very things before us are always transparent. They are both empty and full of possibility.

But what is it necessary to make visible? To begin, we can start with the themes I have raised in this book. The atheist needs to speak to violence, truth, finitude, temporality and our common and universal species-being. The upshot is that this will allow the atheist, as Heidegger saw, to view the human in isolation and as part of a meaningful environment, and as Marx argued, as irrevocably entwined with other instantiations of our species. This, however, must be thought in the broadest possible sense. What the radical atheist has to make apparent is how to appreciate that possibility is always a necessary component of human existence. For the atheist, with her attendant attunement to temporality and finitude, the greatest evil is the subsuming of human beings into absolute nothingness. Non-realized possibilities or potentialities must be avoided at all costs. The atheist must acknowledge the transience of life and the cosmos and yet remain sensitive to that which remains. That is why things, truth, the mortal and the common, in their precarious intransigence, resist formless and unresolved possibilities.

Atheism is that which attends to all that forms and determines protean possibility, exposing and remaining sensitive to how things are created, guided and given purpose within the limits of what reality allows. By now the most straightforward point we should have communicated is that for the atheist, the question of meaning and purpose still has some value. It is not that everything is just some giant cosmic accident and there is nothing of value. In fact now, the opposite is the case: meaning is everywhere. This is not to say it is nowhere, but rather to assert that significance is a lot more palpable in innumerable contexts. The key is that possibility cannot be forsaken. Indeed, the diminishment of human possibility to greater or lesser degrees is an index of barbarism. This requires discourse on many fronts: with regard to the open manifestation of the self in relation to others, in depersonalizing the self and coming to see actions as Sartre would, as a presentation of what humanity ought to be, in seeing human awareness as emerging out of the natural world, of making visible how humans are connected in order to participate in the complex and ongoing history of human existence.[53]

Notes

1   I take this term 'radical atheism' to be a very qualified radicalization of humanism, and in a very specific sense. I use the term radical atheism rather than radical humanism in order to avoid the inflection of its current mainstream deployment, which is to say as an appendage to secular and scientific humanism. However, when I use the term radical atheism I am simply saying that lived human existence ought to be a core concern for any atheism worthy of the name. In a way, I am following Jean Amery in his collection *Radical Humanism: Selected Essays,* trans. Sidney and Stella P. Rosenfeld, (Bloomington: Indiana U.P., 1984), where humanism is thought to require a transformation to respond to the historical problems of the day. Of course, for Amery the issue to which it was pivotal to respond was the Holocaust; any humanism can only ever be meaningful when historical events force us to ask the most fundamental questions regarding human existence and what it can achieve. The term radical atheism was used by Douglas Adams, and has recently been adapted to great effect in a philosophical context by Martin Hägglund. The use of the term stems, I would argue, from a general dissatisfaction common among continental philosophers with the term 'humanism,' as best represented by the atheist humanism practised by the noble humanist associations around the world. For an example of what I mean, see the mission statement of the British Humanist Association http://humanism.org.uk/. The basic point is that radical atheism opposes at the core, and radicalizes where relevant, the tenets of secular humanism. Secular humanism remains too negative, whoever its various interlocutors may be, and does not quite offer engaging enough intellectual material

for making apparent the structure of human existence, its genesis and ethical development. Generally, it should be noted that as an intellectual constellation, the radicalization of humanism is evident in various strands of twentieth-century French thought as exemplified in anti-humanism. The common denominator of these trends in thinkers – philosophers as diverse as Sartre, Malraux, Blanchot, Merleau-Ponty, Derrida, Badiou and Deleuze to name but a few – is that the basic appreciation of that which is human cannot be constrained to the natural and ahistorical. Humanity is simply not individual, innate, or even possessed of inalienable rights. There is no humanity in itself which is not the product of external forces and historical processes. For a wide-ranging discussion of these issues see Stefenos Geroulanos' *An Atheism that is not Humanist Emerges in French Thought*, (Stanford: Stanford U.P., 2010). For a strong account of how atheism has been reconfigured in the latter part of the twentieth century see Christopher Watkin, *Difficult Atheism: Post-Theological Thinking in Alain Badiou, Quentin Meillassoux, and Jean-Luc Nancy*, (Edinburgh: Edinburgh U.P., 2013).

2   Stephen Hawking, *The Grand Design* (London: Bantam, 2011), p.13.

3   Friedrich Nietzsche, *The Gay Science*, trans. W. Kaufman (London: Vintage, 1974), pp.181-182.

4   This reading is suggested and developed by Ullrich Haase in his excellent book *Starting with Nietzsche* (London: Continuum, 2008). Haase develops what is effectively a Heideggerean reading of Nietzsche. Any reflections herein on the relations between Nietzsche and temporality are owed to this interpretation and all errors on my part can be attributed to the author of the aforementioned text.

5   Nietzsche, *Untimely Meditations*, trans. R. Hollingdale (Cambridge, Cambridge U.P., 1983), p.162. Henceforth *UM*.

6   See Nietzsche, *UM*, pp.164-165.

7   See Haase, *Starting with Nietzsche*, pp.9-16 for an approach to Nietzsche that thinks beyond the common canard that Nietzsche argues for the position that all perspectives are equal. While Nietzsche is often cursorily dismissed as the arch-perspectivist, this is an evaluation easily undermined. To suggest that Nietzsche endorses one perspective as being good as another or that truth is dependent on one's perspective only endorses isolated and self-contained clusters of epistemic meaning. There is nothing so distasteful to Nietzsche as the breaking of knowledge into different perspectives such as the scientist's truth, the artist's truth, the archaeologist's truth, the philologist's truth. Such fragmentation only weakens humans' attempt to formulate meaning in life by undermining the exposure of these identities to each other. The point is that truth is not something that is 'there,' like an object. Truth is created, not solely by humans, but with the ebb and flow of natural and historical processes. To suggest 'truth' is isolated to regional discourses is to undermine our understanding of the actual forces of life. For example, see Nietzsche, *Will to Power*, trans. W. Kaufman (New York, Vintage, 1968), p.298-99 (henceforth, WP). While this position is one that could certainly be debated, it is surely something to be taken up in another context.

8   Nietzsche, *WP*, p.19.

9   Nietzsche, *WP*, 20.

10 Nietzsche, *WP*, p.28.

11 Pierre Klossowski, *Nietzsche and the Vicious Circle*, trans. D.W. Smith (London: Continuum, 2005), p. 21.

12 See Klossowski, p.21-24.

13 Nietzsche, *WP*, p.36.

14 Nietzsche, *WP*, pp.38-39.

15 Vladimir Nabokov, *Novels 1969-1974* (New York: Library of

America), p.489.

16 This is an old position mainly articulated by Plato in the *Symposium*. See Plato, Symposium, trans C. Gill (London: Penguin, 1999), p.45. For a systematic modern account of this see Martha Nussbaum's *The Fragility of Goodness* (Cambridge: Cambridge U.P., 2001), pp.165-199.

17 See Maurice Blanchot, *The Work of Fire*, trans. Charlotte Mandell (Stanford: Stanford U.P., 1995), p.344.

18 See Blanchot, *The Infinite Conversation*, trans. Susan Hanson (Minneapolis: University of Minnesota Press), p.145.

19 See Miles Kennedy's *Home: Towards a Bachelardian Concrete Metaphysics* (Bern: Peter Lang, 2011) for an excellent reflection on the metaphysical potential of beginnings.

20 This is a reflection on Sartre's division of the 'for-itself' and the 'in-itself.' J.P. Sartre, *Being and Nothingness: An Essay on Phenomenological Ontology*, trans. Hazel Barnes (London: Routledge, 2003), 119-125. Henceforth *BN*.

21 Jean-Paul Sartre, *BN*, pp.127-129.

22 Ray Brassier, *Nihil Unbound* (Basingstoke: Palgrave, 2010), p.xi.

23 "When I consider the brief span of my life, swallowed up in the eternity before and behind it, the small space that I fill, or even see, engulfed in the infinite immensity of spaces which I know not, and which know not me, I am afraid, and wonder to see myself here rather than there; for there is no reason why I should be here rather than there, now, rather than then." Blaise Pascal, *Pensees*, trans. W.F. Trotter (Seattle: Pacific Publishing, 2010), p.28.

24 See Haase, *Starting with Nietzsche*, p. 30.

25 Martin Hägglund, *Radical Atheism: Derrida and the Time of Life* (Stanford, Stanford U.P., 2008), p.8.

26 For a useful account of how Heidegger radicalizes the question of temporality see H.G. Gadamer's *Truth and Method*, trans. J. Weinsheimer and D.G. Marshall (London:

Continuum, 2004), pp.246-247.

27 See Hägglund's rendition of the logical structure of radical atheism in "Radical Atheist Materialism: A Critique of Meillassoux," *The Speculative Turn: Continental Materialism and Realism*, ed. L. Bryant, G. Harman, and N. Srincek (Melbourne: Re: Press, 2011), pp.114-129.

28 Martin Heidegger, *On Time and Being*, trans. J. Stambaugh (Chicago: University of Chicago Press, 2002), p. 14. Henceforth *TB*.

29 "We cannot attribute the presencing to be thus thought to one of the three dimensions of time, to the present, which would seem obvious. Rather, the unity of time's three dimensions consists in the interplay of each toward each. This interplay proves to be the true extending, playing in the very heart of time, the fourth dimension, so to speak-not only so to speak, but in the nature of the matter. True time is four-dimensional." Heidegger, *TB*, p.15.

30 Heidegger, *Phenomenological Interpretations of Aristotle*, trans. R. Rojcewicz (Bloomington, Indiana U.P.), p.13. Henceforth *PIA*.

31 Heidegger, *PIA*, p.148. This point is, to be fair, ambiguous in Heidegger; Heidegger makes many contradictory statements to the effect that philosophy itself is ontotheology. Philosophy thinks Being both as the most ubiquitous and common as well as potentially the most exemplary being. In addition, much of his *Beiträge* is mystical in outlook. These clearly are not the conventional *causa sui* of metaphysical theology, but the assignation of essential atheism does not easily fit either. For my purposes, I argue that it is possible to take Heidegger as an opening through which a radically atheistic thinking can emerge.

32 Heidegger, *Being and Time*, J. Macquarrie and E. Robinson (New York: Harper & Row, 1962), pp. 377-378. Henceforth *BT*.

33 Heidegger, *BT*, p.380.

34 Heidegger, *BT*, pp.385-388.

35 Heidegger, *BT*, p.358.

36 David Webster, *Dispirited: How Contemporary Capitalism makes us Stupid Selfish and Unhappy* (London: Zero Books, 2012), p.70.

37 Obviously this is not the case for the central thrust of Marxism.

38 Virno places this commonality firmly within the paradoxes and contradictions of Post-Fordist capitalist economics. He defines how the collective moment of capitalist labour such as the factory, information, and public offers opportunities for thinking how a new sense of the 'multitude' might emerge. This is the 'communism of capital'. See Virno, *A Grammar of the Multitude* (Cambridge, MA: MIT Press, 2004), p.110-111. Hereafter *GM*.

39 See Virno, *GM*, pp.76-80.

40 Virno, *GM*, p.77.

41 These of course are deployed in a very specific way for Virno within the particular economic coordinates of Post-Fordism. Virno, *GM*, p.77.

42 Karl Marx, *Economic and Philosophical Manuscripts 1844*, trans. M. Milligan (New York, Dover Publications, 2007), pp.74-77. Henceforth *EPM*.

43 Marx, *EPM*, p.74.

44 Marx, *EPM*, pp.74-75.

45 It is noteworthy that Marx discerned the limitations of the 'physiocrats' too. In some sense Enlightenment materialism is valuable, but it can only become truly valuable when it coincides with a humanism of the practical sphere. See Karl Marx, "French Materialism," in *Selected Writings* (New York: Classic Books International, 2010), p.99.

46 See Jacques Rancière, *On the Shores of Politics* (London: Verso, 2007), p.90-92.

47 Sartre, *Existentialism & Humanism* (London: Metheun, 1973), p. 46. Henceforth EH.

48 "There is no difference between free being – being as self-committal, as existence choosing its essence – and absolute being. And there is no difference whatever between being as an absolute, temporarily localized, that is, localised in history – and universally intelligible being." Sartre, *EH*, p.47.

49 Sartre, *EH*, p.32.

50 It is often claimed that Sartre merely follows a Kantian line here; this is far from the truth. Kant remains too abstract for Sartre, willing an abstract and formal universal. Instead, for Sartre, the universal is action itself. See Sartre, *EH*, p.52.

51 For example, see Camus, *The Rebel*, trans. Anthony Bower (Harmondsworth: Penguin, 1962), pp. 173-192.

52 We think of the mess of purposive and non-purposive human agency, in an engaged and caring sense that lives the ecstatic truth of the world, without remaining concerned with the lazy critiques of postmodernism as self-creative, self-fashioning and so forth.

53 Along with Stephen Hawking, I would like to thank the Philosophy students in Phil 203 at Nottingham Trent University for their contribution to the ideas discussed in this book. I would also like to thank David Webster, Matthew Bernard and especially Ruth O'Connor for the comments they have made on various drafts of the manuscript.

BOOKS

Iff Books is interested in ideas and reasoning. It publishes material on science, philosophy and law. Iff Books aims to work with authors and titles that augment our understanding of the human condition, society and civilisation, and the world or universe in which we live.